Seeing Smart Cities Through
a Multi-Dimensional Lens

H. Patricia McKenna

Seeing Smart Cities Through a Multi-Dimensional Lens

Perspectives, Relationships, and Patterns for Success

 Springer

H. Patricia McKenna
Victoria, BC, Canada

ISBN 978-3-030-70823-8   ISBN 978-3-030-70821-4   (eBook)
https://doi.org/10.1007/978-3-030-70821-4

This Springer imprint is published by the registered company Springer Nature Switzerland AG
The registered company address is: Gewerbestrasse 11, 6330 Cham, Switzerland

Foreword

In our early days in the doctoral program at Syracuse University, I was drawn to Dr. Patricia McKenna's passion for understanding and contributing to the potential of people to work in concert with information and communication technologies in unique and innovative ways. At our first meeting as a cohort, we were asked to share our research interests. Patricia was interested in the ambient dimension of information and communication—I was intrigued and thankful to be sitting alongside this classmate, then colleague, and today, friend and fellow researcher. Our conversations in lounges, coffee shops, and walking down the street were stimulating and hopeful—at the core of our discussions was the potential for new and emerging technologies to support collaboration, learning, and well-being. Over the past 10 years, I have had the pleasure of collaborating with Dr. McKenna on research projects and an ambitious grant proposal; still, it is simply conversing about her deep commitment to her research space that I find both motivating and satisfying. Her research is substantial. Her work contributes to and benefits the wider community.

In this book, Dr. McKenna shares a holistic perspective of success in smart cities by organizing and reframing varied research lenses and components. Each chapter considers what smartness looks like, feels like, and sounds like. She shares that at the core of successful smart cities and regions is the motivated engagement of aware people working with aware technologies. In her conversational style and with an authoritative voice, she invites readers to bring their own thoughts and questions into the conversation. Most importantly, we are invited to consider challenges, practices, and future research as options to build on her work. One of the key challenges she points to is the potential of open data versus concerns about data privacy. This issue is revisited in multiple chapters. We are reminded that open data sharing can have both positive and negative consequences. Individuals and organizations are becoming more thoughtful about what they choose to share and with whom. For example, concerns about sharing personally identifiable information have brought more stringent controls to the education sector with new policies impacting both educators and vendors of learning technologies.

While the chapters can stand alone and be read in any order, connections are likely to emerge and speak to an individual's particular experiences and interests. Using a case study approach which "incorporates multiple methods of data collection...combined with an explanatory correlational design," the first eight chapters explore six dimensions of smart cities—sensing, awareness, learning, openness, innovation, and disruption. In the final chapter, McKenna deftly reveals the interconnections among these dimensions. As intended, the interests of diverse audiences are addressed—government agencies, community organizers, educators, and those who are responsible for building the infrastructures that make spaces safe, inviting, and accessible. Cross-sector collaboration is a key goal in smart places and spaces, wherein the interests and knowledge of varied audiences come together to innovate, create, and disrupt.

In this ambitious, accessible book, Dr. McKenna teases apart and then reconceives the multidimensional relationships that emerge when aware people work in concert with aware technologies in places and spaces that become "smarter" as a result of participatory, motivated engagement of informed citizens.

In appreciation for your commitment to excellence as a researcher and in your willingness to welcome others to journey with you to discover new opportunities for aware people to engage with aware technologies to learn and foster well-being.

Biography. I am curious about the multiplicity of factors that support learning in formal and informal settings. My research considers these factors through various lenses and perspectives—motivation, curiosity, creativity, environment, sociotechno, socio-cultural, and cultural-historical. I draw on theoretical frameworks—motivation theories and models—and conceptual frameworks—activity theory, systems and design thinking—to support identification and analysis of opportunities to create frictionless, face-to-face, virtual, and blended learning environments. I conceived the concept of "frictionless learning environments" as the integration of optimally structured space, time, resources, and community interaction to support achievement of individual and group learning goals. Environment is considered from an external context and internal context perspective. My current work centers around merging teaching, learning, and assessment into collaborative, responsive digital spaces. Learn more about my work at www.informationconnections.com.

District Superintendent/CEO   Dr. Sarah A. Chauncey
Rockland BOCES
West Nyack, NY, USA

Preface

This book was written to shed light on the many perspectives involved in providing an understanding of smart cities and regions. With smart cities encompassing a wide range of domains, it has been difficult for researchers and practitioners to provide a unified and comprehensive definition. Beginning with an exploration of the research literature for smart cities, this book identifies several dimensions that form the focus of this work—sensing, awareness, learning, openness, innovation, and disruption. These six dimensions associated with smart cities are then developed and operationalized to form a conceptual framework for seeing through smart cities. While many books provide descriptions of technologies in smart cities and others provide utopian or dystopian visions of smart cities, this book instead explores a range of perspectives on smart cities and offers an analysis of components contributing to the potential for success. Although there are a range of smart city guides where reference is made to correlation for predictive purposes in relation to crime, for planning and financial forecasting, informing public safety, and the like, this book focuses on explanatory correlational design in identifying and testing a wide range of everyday, experience-related aspects of urban life, with implications for the imagining and design of living environments. As such, through the identification of patterns and relationships in contemporary urban environments, this book is focused on developing starting points for understanding factors contributing to the success of smart city projects as well as broader initiatives contributing to livability as a key outcome for success. Additionally, this book uses the metaphor of "seeing through" to advance and provide interpretations and ways of seeing for improving understandings of smart cities. Responding to the need for more case studies and empirical research, this book also seeks to identify emerging factors that are contributing to the making and evolving of smart cities from the perspective of people living in urban environments and regions, providing a real world view and a window or lens into the smart cities phenomenon. This book is based on evidence gathered from a wide range of people in small- to medium- to large-sized cities, in countries spanning several continents—from North America (e.g., Canada and the United States), to Europe (from Ireland in the North to Greece in the South), extending to the Middle East (Israel).

The intended audience for this book encompasses urban practitioners and researchers seeking to improve their understanding of the smart city concept while the componential framework is intended to provide a guide for those involved with smart city initiatives, and for those concerned with factors contributing to the potential for success. As such, the audience for this book includes community members, leaders, planners, and developers; city governments; and academics, students, and researchers. This book is also intended to be used as a textbook for college and university courses that focus on the study of smart cities and regions and as a resource for community leaders in urban communities and regions. As such, this book has the potential to be used as a textbook for courses in a wide range of domains (e.g., environmental design, human geography, innovation, urban planning) and will also be of interest to educators designing courses for affective computing, sociology, urban informatics, data analytics, to name a few. Indeed, three questions are provided at the end of each chapter for educators, students, and community leaders. Readers of this book are encouraged to share their responses to these questions with the author of this book through a link to an online space that is provided. In short, this book will be of interest to a diverse audience, from those launching smart city initiatives; to those seeking guidance on the evaluation and assessment of cities and urban regions for smartness; to those seeking emerging predictors of success for smart cities, learning cities, and future cities.

The organization of this book consists of three parts and nine chapters as described in the following paragraphs. Part I consists of three chapters and focuses on smart city perspectives, spaces for people, and a hybrid study approach. Chapter 1 provides an introduction and background to perspectives on smart cities along with evolving definitions. The focus and research questions and propositions to be explored in the remainder of the book are also identified. Chapter 2 provides an exploration of the sensing dimension, using an exploratory case study approach, involving people and their multi-sensorial capabilities in the form of emotion/affect (e.g., comfort), as acting and influencing in smart cities, in creating possibly novel and meaningful spaces for people. Chapter 3 provides a hybrid approach to seeing through smart cities by providing a rationale for the combining of an explanatory correlational design with an exploratory case study research approach.

Building upon the approach developed in Chaps. 2 and 3, Part II consists of four chapters and focuses on emerging urban patterns and relationships influencing and informing smart cities. Chapter 4 explores the awareness dimension as a way of seeing through smart cities focusing on people and data. Urban interactions are explored in relation to elements such as the use of information and communications technologies (ICTs) and access to public data. Chapter 5 explores the learning dimension and data in smart cities, focusing on community participation and data-related elements such as privacy, security, and trust, along with the importance of visual ways to show success. Chapter 6 explores the openness dimension and data access in smart cities in relation to privacy, trust, and connecting and the notion of infrastructures for openness. Chapter 7 explores the innovation dimension and data in smart cities in terms of creative opportunities, meaningfulness associated with factors contributing to increased value for data, and potential uses for data.

Part III consists of two chapters and focuses on complexity, disruptiveness, and transformation in smart cities. Chapter 8 explores the disruption dimension in smart cities and regions in relation to cross-sector collaborations and visualizations of data to inform, educate, and inspire in real time, in seeking to navigate pathways and directions for success. Chapter 9 provides a synthesis of the book and an analysis while offering opportunities for seeing potentials for success in smart cities. Based on findings from the explorations and correlations conducted across the chapters of the book, a typology for seeing through smart cities is developed, opening spaces for the evolving of urban theory and smart cities theory going forward.

Each chapter in this book is intended to stand on its own, and it is for this reason that the description of the methodology may appear to repeat across multiple chapters (e.g., Chaps. 4–8). In exploring the six dimensions for seeing through smart cities in this book, a template is introduced in Chap. 1 and is used in each of the following chapters. The template is used to highlight the key challenges and opportunities based on the research literature for both practice and research. The template is also used to highlight insights, patterns, spaces for dialogue, and urban theory and methods, based on exploratory case study and explanatory correlational design findings.

Key topic areas for this work include the following:

Aware people
Aware technologies
Awareness
Correlation
Creativity
Disruption
Equity and inclusion
Future cities
Innovation
Learning cities
Openness
Patterns
Relationships
Sensing
Urban data and access, privacy, security, and trust
Urban experiences
Urban interactions

Acknowledgment and appreciation for the support and assistance in preparing the book are extended to Springer staff as well as to the multiple peer reviewers who provided highly valuable guidance for this book and to the many individuals who participated in the underlying study for this work. Special thanks to Dr. Sarah Chauncey for contributing a Foreword to this book.

A very special thanks to Jeanine, Harper, and Boone for their support, guidance, and inspiration.

Victoria, BC, Canada   H. Patricia McKenna

Contents

Abbreviations

AI	Artificial intelligence
BIM	Building Information Modelling
BIS	Body insight scale
COVID-19	Coronavirus disease 2019
FG-SSC	Focus Group on Smart Sustainable Cities
HCI	Human–computer interaction
ICTs	Information and communication technologies
IFDS	Institute for Foundations of Data Science
ISA	International Sociological Association
IoT	Internet of Things
IT	Information technology
ITU	International Telecommunications Union
JCA-IoT and SC&C	Joint Coordination Activity on Internet of Things and Smart Cities and Communities
LOTC	Language of the city
RC21	Research Committee 21 on Sociology of Urban and Regional Development of the ISA
SCC	Smart Cities Council
SCs	Smart cities
UNESCO	United Nations Educational, Scientific and Cultural Organization
UTL	Urban Theory Lab
VR	Virtual reality

Part I
Smart City Perspectives, Spaces for People, and a Hybrid Study Approach

Chapter 1
Perspectives on Smart Cities

An Introduction and Background

1.1 Introduction

The research literature for the smart city phenomenon points to an ongoing emergence and evolving of the smartness concept [1] throughout the first decade of the twenty-first century, indicating that we are now in the third decade of development. Cohen [2] speaks of smart city development in terms of waves or generations where the first generation was mostly about the technologies; the second generation was "technology enabled" and "city-led"; and the third generation is about involving people and is referred to as "citizen co-creation" where a blend of all three generations is encouraged. Other researchers [3] identify the move "beyond the last decade's conception of smart cities and urban computing" while advancing "a deeper level of symbiosis among smart cities, internet of things, and ambient spaces." Pushing further still is the move to Societies 5.0 [4] as a "people-centric super-smart society." Through a review of the research literature for smart cities, the focus of this work is on ways of seeing from multiple disciplinary perspectives in relation to emerging technologies [5], urban theory [6] and frameworks [7, 8], people and their interactions in real time [3], along with associated challenges and opportunities enabled through highly disruptive [9] and contested developments [10] in urban environments and regions. Concerns are expressed in the world more generally in relation to "smartglasses" [11] for example, where it is said that we could "quite literally" be "seeing the world through Apple's lens" by "putting a digital layer between us and the world" giving rise to "privacy concerns" and "deeper questions" pertaining to "what our relationship should be to a technology that mediates our every interaction with the world" [11].

© Springer Nature Switzerland AG 2021
H. P. McKenna, *Seeing Smart Cities Through a Multi-Dimensional Lens*
https://doi.org/10.1007/978-3-030-70821-4_1

1.2 Background

By way of background, this section provides additional context through definitions in Sect. 1.2.1 for key terms used in this work, based on the research literature and the identification of objectives for this work in Sect. 1.2.2.

1.2.1 Definitions

Definitions for the smart cities concept are provided based on perspectives emerging from the research literature for smart cities and regions. Definitions for key terms used in this work are then provided and focus on the words: perceive, see, seeing, and transparent. Also presented are definitions for urban theory and ambient theory in relation to smart cities.

Smart Cities

Perspective 1—Information Technology to Address Problems Townsend [5] describes smart cities as "places where information technology is combined with infrastructure, architecture, everyday objects and even our bodies, to address social, economic, and environmental problems."

Perspective 2—ICTs, Quality of Life, and Sustainability Habitat III, The United Nations Conference on Housing and Sustainable Urban Development [12] released a series of issue papers, one of which focuses on smart cities, acknowledging the many definitions of the concept, providing different understandings "by different people and sectors" from smart as intelligent in relation to "physical, social, institutional, and economic infrastructure while ensuring centrality of citizens in a sustainable environment" to those characterized by "smart economy, smart mobility, smart people, smart environment, smart living, smart governance" [12], to those concerned with "the strategic use of new technology and innovative approaches to enhance the efficiencies and competitiveness of cities" [12]. These definitions are encompassed perhaps in the definition of a smart sustainable city advanced by the International Telecommunications Union (ITU), Focus Group on Smart Sustainable Cities (FG-SSC) as "an innovative city that uses ICTs and other means to improve the quality of life, efficiency of urban operations and services, and competitiveness, while ensuring that it meets the needs of present and future generations with respect of economic, social and environmental aspects" [12]. It is worth noting that more recently the ITU formed an entity referred to as Joint Coordination Activity on Internet of Things and Smart Cities and Communities (JCA-IoT and SC&C) [13].

Perspective 3—Evolving Understandings focusing on Human-Centric, Social, and Economic Deguchi [14] notes that, "the definition of *smart city* has changed over time and will continue to shift" where, Japan uses the "Society 5.0 vision" that "encapsulates innovation driven for and from robotics, AI, IoT and big data" and as such, "challenge technologies to create new social contracts and economic models in a more human-centric manner." Emphasizing a social dimension, the H-UTokyo Lab [4] advances "Society 5.0"in Japan. An article in Forbes [15] claims that "smart cities are windows into the future" and as such, they "revitalize communities by considering how to improve human living spaces and values over time."

Perspective 4—A Technology, Data, and People Interactive Dynamic Willis and Aurigi [16] offer a definition of 'smart city' in three parts, and reminiscent of the three generations identified by Cohen [2], as: first "the emergence of new ways in which material urban systems are interconnected through information and data"; second, "changes in the processes through which cities are monitored, managed and analyzed" and third, "a shift in how citizens participate, interact with the city and inhabit its spaces."

Perceive, See, Seeing, and Transparent

Definitions are explored for other key terms in this work including perceive, see, seeing, and transparent.

Perceive The Merriam-Webster Thesaurus [17] describes perceive as "to make note of (something) through the use of one's eyes" and "to have a clear idea of."

See The Cambridge English Dictionary [18] defines *see* as "to be conscious of what is around you by using your eyes." The Merriam-Webster Thesaurus [19] defines *see* as "to come to a knowledge of (something) by living through it" or "to come to an awareness of" or "to have a clear idea of" and identifies a range of synonyms for see as: appreciate, apprehend, assimilate, behold, catch on (to), cognize, comprehend, conceive, decipher, decode, dig, discern, get, grasp, intuit, know, make out, perceive, recognize, register, savvy, seize, sense, twig, understand. The Merriam-Webster Thesaurus [19] also defines *see* as "to form a mental picture of" while identifying synonyms as: conceive, conjure (up), dream, envisage, envision, fancy, fantasize, ideate, image, imagine, picture, vision, visualize."

Seeing The Merriam-Webster Thesaurus [20] defines *seeing* as "to make note of (something) through the use of one's eyes" and synonyms are identified as: "beholding, catching, discerning, distinguishing, noticing, observing, regarding, spotting, spying, viewing, witnessing." The Merriam-Webster Thesaurus [20] also defines *seeing* as "to have a clear idea of" and synonyms are identified as: "appreciating, apprehending, assimilating, comprehending, conceiving" to name a few.

Transparent The Merriam-Webster Thesaurus [21] describes transparent as "easy to see through" while noting the close relationships with translucence.

Urban and Ambient Theory

This work is attentive to urban theory as defined in relation to ambient theory in the context of increasingly aware and pervasive technologies.

Urban Theory Researchers at the Urban Theory Lab [22] challenge "inherited frameworks of urban knowledge" as in, "the urban/suburban/rural distinction" arguing that they "must be radically reinvented" in order "to illuminate emergent forms of twenty-first urbanization" where "all political-economic and socio-environmental relations are enmeshed, regardless of terrestrial location or morphological configuration" as in, "planetary urbanization."

Ambient Theory Enabled by increasingly aware people and aware technologies, this work further advances the need for ambient theory [23] to accommodate more dynamic, adaptive, and contextual interactions and to complement existing and evolving urban theory. Indeed, Rickert [24] provides an interpretation of the ambient as "seeing that which surrounds and encompasses as also gifting and guiding us."

1.2.2 Objectives

Key objectives for this chapter include (a) providing an overview of evolving perspectives on the smart cities concept; (b) developing a conceptual framework for seeing through smart cities and regions; and (c) identifying propositions, based on the conceptual framework presented, for exploration in the chapters that follow in this book.

1.3 Seeing through Smart Cities: A Theoretical Perspective

The smart cities concept is explored and developed through a review of the research literature in relation to emerging technologies, urban theory, people, and disruptive and contested initiatives. Focus is placed on perspectives and the notion of seeing, so that theoretically, this work is situated at the intersection of the notion of seeing in the context of smart cities and the associated challenges and opportunities.

1.3.1 Emerging Technologies & Smart Cities

Johnson [25] considers "the transformation" that "density" assisted in bringing about by "building cities with populations in the millions" giving rise to the need for "sharing the same water supply, struggling to find a way to get rid of all that human waste and animal waste" which, although "turbulent", turn out to be "the most affluent places on the planet, with life expectancies that are nearly double that of predominantly rural nations." According to Johnson [25] density is viewed as "a positive force" as in "an engine of wealth creation, population reduction, environmental sustainability" making us "dependent on dense urban living as a survival strategy." And yet, Johnson [25] acknowledges that "this epic transformation" to a "city-planet where eighty percent of us live in metropolitan areas" is not a given and "could be undone" whereby "new forces could emerge" to "imperil this city-planet of ours" posing the question "But what might they be?" It is worth noting that Johnson [25] speculates that "if some new force derails our migration to the cities, it will take the form of a threat that specifically exploits density to harm us" likening it to the cholera epidemic two centuries ago. If some new virus emerges, and indeed it has with the emergence of COVID-19, Johnson [25] claims that "Combatting this new reality will take a twenty-first century version of Snow's map" thereby "making visible patterns in the daily flow of lives and deaths" and as such, "constitute the metabolism of a city, the rising and falling fortunes of the sick and healthy." Over a decade ago Johnson concluded that "thanks to urban density and global jet travel, it's probably easier for a rogue virus to spread around the globe" while claiming that, "our ability to render a virus harmless is growing at exponential rates" although this seemed questionable in the face of the COVID-19 pandemic throughout 2020 and beyond. From a sustainable urbanism perspective, Lehmann [26] provides three case studies of density in Singapore, Hong Kong, and Vancouver, giving rise to potential for the notion of "optimal density" taking into consideration quality of life and livability. If people spend less time in cities and seek the outer regions to avoid density this gives rise to questions such as: *what is the impact and role of remote working and digital nomads in smart cites?* Nam and Pardo [27] articulated the smart cities concept as a way for cities to innovate in the face of rapid growth using information and communication technologies (ICTs). Batty [6] speaks in terms of high and low frequency cities where change occurs rapidly in the former "over very fine time intervals, seconds, minutes, hours, days" and more slowly in the latter case "over years, decades, centuries."

1.3.2 Urban Theory & Smart Cities

The Urban Theory Lab [22] argues that "the urban today represent a worldwide condition" where "all political-economic and socio-environmental relations are enmeshed." This gives rise to questions such as: *are we experiencing a decentralization away from urban environments?* Batty [6] calls for a reinvigorating of "tools we have been developing for the last half century" to "complement and supplement rather than substitute" urban theory, practices, methods, ideologies, models and the like. Hunter [28], with the notion of "ambient contextuality" where "there is information hidden all around us that helps clarify our intent in any given conversation" nudges us toward the need for urban theory that takes into account the ambient. Mora et al. [29] advance the notion of a middle-range theory of sustainable smart city transitions from an interdisciplinary perspective involving cross-case analysis.

1.3.3   People and Smart Cities

In *Seeing the Better City: How to Explore, Observe, and Improve Urban Space*, Wolfe [8] speaks of the "need to do a better job of finding a role for our human experience" and "awaken our senses" while noting that the likes of Gehl, Jacobs, and Whyte "have also encouraged purposeful consciousness of surroundings through visual and other sensory means." Streitz [30] addresses problems associated with "the smart everything paradigm" in smart cities, proposing "a human-centered design approach" in support of "keeping the human in the loop and in control" such that "smart spaces make people smarter." Willis and Aurigi [16] advance the notion of "smart city visions" enabled through visual models, storytelling, and placemaking.

1.3.4   Disruptive and Contested Nature of Smart City Initiatives

Roy and Ong [10] understand the urban to be "a milieu that is in constant formation" and is "inherently unstable" and "subject to intense contestations" while being "always incomplete." Egyedi and Mehos [31] articulate the disruptiveness of inverse infrastructure as "bottom-up, user-driven, self-organizing networks" using the example of Wikipedia. Finger [9] discusses information and communication technologies (ICTs) in the context of smart cities, as enabling a data layer, that is "substantially changing, if not revolutionizing, the provision of urban infrastructure services" such that digitalization and the combination of associated elements is having a "disruptive effect on absolutely everything." Finger [9] claims for example that "the data layer", as in, information, "can be used to produce new services, new business models" and draw "new customers." Anderson [32] advances the disruptive and contested notion of "the end of theory" with data everywhere available.

Table 1.1 Emerging tech, urban theory, people & disruptiveness by author/year

Author(s)	Year	Emerging tech	Urban theory	People	Disruptiveness
Johnson	2006	Urban density			Digital/data layer
Anderson	2008				End of theory
Nam & Pardo	2011	City innovation			
Roy & Ong	2011				Urban as dynamic
Egyedi & Mehos	2012				Inverse infrastructure
Finger	2016				ICTs & data layer
Lehmann	2016		Optimal density	Livability	
Wolfe	2017			Senses	
Hunter	2018		Ambient context		
Streitz	2018			In the loop	
Batty	2020		High/low frequency		
Mora et al.	2020		SSC transitions		
UTL	2020		Worldwide condition		

1.3.5   Summary

In summary, this review of the literature highlights the importance of seeing in relation to dimensions such as sensing, awareness, learning, openness, innovation, and disruptiveness for smart cities. This theoretical perspective provides a background and context for development, theorizing, and operationalization of a conceptual framework for seeing through smart cities.

Summary In summary, Table 1.1 provides an overview of the research literature for smart cities highlighting the key elements of emerging technologies, urban theory, people, and disruptiveness by author and year.

Regarding emerging technologies, Johnson [25] discusses urban density while Nam and Pardo [27] provide an innovation perspective. For urban theory, Hunter [28] addresses the ambient context, Batty [6] high and low frequency cities, Mora et al. [29] with a middle-range theory of sustainable smart city transitions, and the Urban Theory Lab (UTL) provides an interpretation of cities as a worldwide condition. People are conceptualized by Wolfe [8] in relation to the senses and by Streitz (2018) [30] in terms of awareness and being kept in the loop in smart cities.

Disruptiveness is discussed by Johnson [25] in terms of the digital and data layer; by Anderson [32] in terms of the end of theory in the context of big data; by Roy and Ong [10] in terms of the urban as dynamic; by Egyedi and Mehos [31] in relation to inverse infrastructure; by Finger (2016) through the data layer enabled by information and communication technologies (ICTs); by Lehmann [26] through examples of "optimized quality density" in exploring what might constitute "an ideal density model"; by Wolfe [8] taking into consideration people and their senses; by Streitz (2018) [30] noting the importance of keeping people in the loop; by Hunter [28] with ambient context important for urban theory; by Batty [6] with the notion of high and low frequency cities, influencing urban theory; and by the UTL [22] highlighting the importance of the worldwide condition influencing urban theory.

This overview is not intended to be comprehensive but rather suggestive of the range, breadth, and interdisciplinarity of dimensions associated with understandings of smart cities. Although categorized by emerging technologies, urban theory, people, and disruptiveness, it is important to note that commonalities among researcher perspectives exist within and across categories where the disruptive edges into other categories as well. Other questions embedded is this review pertain to the impact and role of the sharing economy [33] on smart cities.

1.3.6 Conceptual Framework for Seeing Smart Cities Through a Multi-dimensional Lens

The seeing concept is operationalized in this work based on discussions with diverse individuals in the context of learning cities and smart cities about technology-infused city spaces focusing on experiences and assessments by people in relation to their city and region as smart. As illustrated in Fig. 1.1, through the interactive dynamic of *people—technologies—cities,* the notion of seeing smart cities through a multi-dimensional lens is enabled through sensing, awareness, learning, openness, innovation, and disruption as explored in the chapters of this book, contributing to emergent understandings and findings.

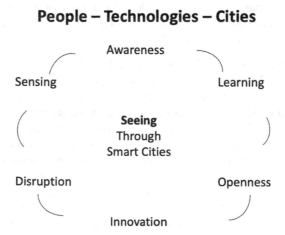

Fig. 1.1 Conceptual framework for seeing smart cities through a multi-dimensional lens

This exploration of seeing through smart cities gives rise to six research questions.

Q1: Why is *sensing* as a way of *seeing* important for people in smart cities? (Chap. 2)
Q2: Why is *awareness* important in relation to the generation of data in smart cities? (Chap. 4)
Q3: How does *learning* pertain to data in smarter city initiatives? (Chap. 5)
Q4: Why does *openness* matter for data access in smart cities? (Chap. 6)
Q5: How does *innovation* as creative opportunity contribute to value in relation to data in the public realm? (Chap. 7)
Q6: Why is *disruptiveness* important for success in smart cities? (Chap. 8)

These six research questions will be addressed in the indicated chapters of this book and will be reformulated as propositions for exploration, as follows.

P1: *Sensing* as a way of *seeing* is important for people in smart cities because this enables light to be shed on experiences, assessments, and visualizations of the urban for understanding, action, and success (Chap. 2)
P2: *Awareness* is important in relation to the generation of data in smart cities in many ways, on many levels, including the use of information and communication technologies (ICTs) and associated issues of privacy and trust (Chap. 4)
P3: *Learning* pertains to data in smarter city initiatives on many levels, across many sectors including learning infrastructures and knowledge infrastructures associated with people and data *privacy*, *security*, and *trust* (Chap. 5)
P4: *Openness* matters for data access in smart cities as data becomes more critical, complex, and valuable requiring ever more creativity associated with policy, governance, regulation, *privacy*, and *connecting* (Chap. 6)
P5: *Innovation* as creative opportunity contributes to value in relation to data in the public realm in terms of potentials for smart cities such as *visual ways to show success in real time* (Chap. 7)
P6: *Disruptiveness* is important for success in smart cities, associated as it is with opportunities for adaptiveness, *collaborations*, and the *use of data to inform, educate, and inspire in real time* (Chap. 8)

In summary, Fig. 1.2 provides an overview of variables for the exploration of seeing, chapter-by-chapter, in relation to urban elements, spaces, and interactions.

1.4   Smart Cities and Associated Challenges and Opportunities

Explorations of seeing through smart cities identifies a range of challenges and opportunities as discussed in Sects. 1.4.1 and 1.4.2.

Variables for Seeing (by Chapter) in Relation to **Urban Elements**

Sensing	Chapter 2	Attuning to Urban Spaces, Walkability, Livability, Interactive public spaces
Awareness	Chapter 4	ICTs, Trust, Privacy
Learning	Chapter 5	Community Participation & Privacy, Security, Trust, Ways to Show Success
Openness	Chapter 6	Access to Public Data, Privacy, Trust, Connecting
Innovation	Chapter 7	Creative Opportunities & Meaningfulness, Access to Public Data Innovative Use of Data & Meaningfulness, Visualize Ways to Show Success
Disruption	Chapter 8	Adapting for Urban Uses & Collaborations, Ways to Show Success Collaborations & Use of Data to Inform, Educate & Inspire in Real Time

Fig. 1.2 Variables for the exploration of seeing through smart cities

1.4.1 Seeing Through Smart Cities and Associated Challenges

On a chapter by chapter basis, this work explores a range of challenges for practice and research associated with seeing through smart cities based on a review of the research and practice literature. Beginning with Chap. 2, challenges associated with *sensing* in smart cities are explored through use of the proxy, *attuning to urban spaces,* in relation to *comfort* as emotion/affect, *walkability, livability* and *interactive public spaces.* Chapter 3 revisits the research design for this book that is used in Chap. 2 and addresses challenges associated with seeing through smart cities and introduces the hybrid exploratory case study and explanatory correlational approach and design as a way of mitigating challenges. Chapter 4 addresses challenges associated with *awareness* in relation to *ICTs* (information and communication technologies) and the generation of data in smart cities. Chapter 5 addresses challenges associated with *learning* in smart cities using *community participation* as a proxy, in relation to *privacy,* to *security,* and to *trust.* Chapter 6 addresses challenges associated with *openness* in smart cities in relation to *access to public data.* Chapter 7 addresses challenges associated with *innovation* in smart cities through use of *creative opportunities* as a proxy in relation to *meaningfulness* as well as to *visualizing ways to show success in real time.* Chapter 8 addresses challenges associated with *disruptiveness* in smart cities through use of *adapting for urban uses* as a proxy in relation to *cross-sector collaboration* and for *visualizations of data to inform, educate, and inspire in real time.*

1.4.2   Seeing Through Smart Cities and Associated Opportunities

On a chapter by chapter basis, this work explores a range of opportunities for practice and research associated with seeing through smart cities, based on the study underlying this work. In Chap. 2, opportunities associated with *sensing* in smart cities are explored in relation to *attuning to urban spaces* and to infrastructures, both visible and less visible. Chapter 3 revisits the research design for this book and addresses opportunities associated with a hybrid exploratory case study and explanatory correlational design approach in support of explorations for seeing through smart cities using the findings from Chap. 2 on the sensing dimension. Chapter 4 explores opportunities associated with *awareness* in relation to ICTs and data generation in smart cities. Chapter 5 explores opportunities associated with *learning* in relation to *data privacy, security,* and *trust* in smart cities. Chapter 6 explores opportunities associated with *openness* in relation to *access to public data* in smart cities. Chapter 7 explores opportunities associated with *innovation* using *creative opportunities* as a proxy in relation to *meaningfulness* as well as to *visualizing ways to show success in real time* in smart cities. Chapter 8 explores opportunities associated with *disruptiveness* in smart cities using *adapting for urban uses* as a proxy in relation to *cross-sector collaboration* and for *visual ways to show success in real time.* Chapter 9 provides a synthesis of the book, identifying opportunities for success, change, transformation, and the value of a typology for smart cities enabled through ways of seeing through smart cities.

1.4.3   Methodology

The methodology for this book consists of an exploratory case study design involving the use of survey and in-depth interviews for the collection of data about smart cities and regions. Again, as indicated in Sect. 1.3.6 of this chapter, the study underlying this work is based on the experiences and assessments of a diverse array of people in multiple cities and countries, in relation to their city and region as smart. This design is described in more detail in Chap. 2 where it is implemented and then again in Chap. 3 where it is revisited and enriched to include a hybrid approach involving the use of an explanatory correlational design.

1.5   Explorations for Practice and Research

For each chapter, challenges and opportunities for explorations of seeing through smart cities are identified for practice and research, contributing to insights that may inform future directions, identify patterns, create spaces for dialogue going forward, and contribute to urban theory, as depicted in the template in Table. 1.2.

Table 1.2 Challenges & opportunities for explorations of seeing through smart cities

	Practice	Research
Challenges	Challenge 1	Challenge 1
	Challenge 2	Challenge 2
	Challenge 3	Challenge 3
Opportunities	Opportunity 1	Opportunity 1
	Opportunity 2	Opportunity 2
	Opportunity 3	Opportunity 3

Insights	
Patterns	
Spaces for dialogue	
Urban theory & methods	

1.6 Conclusion

This chapter provides an introduction to the multidimensional perspectives on smart cities based on a review of the research and practice literature. Focus is placed on emerging technologies, urban theory, people, and the disruptive and contested nature of smart city initiatives and understandings. Using insights emerging from the literature review, the conceptual framework for seeing smart cities through a multi-dimensional lens is developed and operationalized for use in this work. The framework guides the explorations conducted in the chapters that follow using the various six dimensions—*sensing, awareness, learning, openness, innovation*, and *disruption*. These component dimensions are explored in relation to smart city elements such as *walkability, livability, comfort, interactive public spaces, ICTs, data privacy, data security, trust, access to public data, meaningfulness, visualizing ways to show success, cross-sector collaboration,* and *visualizations of data to inform, educate, and inspire in real time.* The framework is also intended to be used for exploring and developing theory in the context of smart cities, learning cities, and future cities. The main contributions of this chapter include the following: (a) development and operationalization of a conceptual framework for seeing smart cities through a multi-dimensional lens (b) extending the research and practice literature for smart cities; and (c) extending theory and frameworks for smart cities. A key takeaway from this chapter is the role of people in seeing through smart cities as a form of human infrastructure, complementing physical and digital infrastructures in urban areas and regions. This work will be of interest to a broad audience including educators, city officials, business, community members and leaders, urban designers and planners, city staff, students, smart city researchers and practitioners, and anyone concerned with understanding smart cities enabled by seeing through smart cities, in support of learning cities and future cities and regions. As such, three questions are raised for educators, students, and community leaders, as follows:

Q 1.1. What would you say is missing from this introduction to perspectives on smart cities as a background for seeing through smart cities?

Q 1.2. How would you describe the notion of seeing through smart cities?

Q 1.3. Is it important to find ways of seeing through smart cities and regions? Please explain briefly why or why not.

If you would like to share your responses to these questions with the author of this book an online space is provided here [https://forms.gle/bJyKeyvtFmnpfFgEA].

References

1. Scholl, H. J. (2016). Foreword. In J. R. Gil-Garcia, T. A. Pardo, & T. Nam (Eds.), *Smarter as the new urban agenda: A comprehensive view of the 21st century city. Public administration and information technology* (Vol. 11). Cham: Springer.
2. Cohen, B. (2015). The 3 generations of smart cities: Inside the development of the technology driven city. *Fast Company Magazine*. Retrieved July 7, 2020, from https://www.fastcompany.com/3047795/the-3-generations-of-smart-cities
3. Konomi, S., & Roussos, G. (2017). *Enriching urban spaces with ambient computing, the internet of things, and smart city design*. Hershey, PA: IGI Global.
4. Hitachi-UTokyo Lab. (2020). *Society 5.0: A people-centric super-smart society*. Singapore: Springer.
5. Townsend, A. M. (2013). *Smart cities: Big data, civic hackers and the quest for a new utopia*. New York: WW Norton.
6. Batty, M. (2020). Defining smart cities: High and low frequency cities, big data and urban theory. In K. S. Willis & A. Aurigi (Eds.), *The Routledge companion to smart cities* (pp. 51–60). London: Routledge.
7. Charoubi, H., Nam, T., Walker, S., Gil-Garcia, J. R., Mellouli, S., Nahon, K., ... Scholl, H. J. (2012). Understanding smart cities: An integrative framework. In *Proc of the 45th HICSS* (pp. 2289–2297).
8. Wolfe, C. R. (2017). *Seeing the better city: How to explore, observe, and improve urban space*. Washington, DC: Island Press.
9. Finger, M. (2016). *Smart cities—Management of smart urban infrastructures. (Massive Open Online Course)*. Lausanne: École Polytechnique Fédérale de Lausanne.
10. Roy, A., & Ong, A. (Eds.). (2011). *Worlding cities: Asian experiments and the art of being global*. Oxford: Wiley-Blackwell. https://doi.org/10.1002/9781444346800
11. Hern, A. (2020). How big tech got bigger, part human, part machine: Is apple turning us all into cyborgs? *The Guardian*. Retrieved November 25, 2020, from https://www.theguardian.com/technology/2020/nov/25/part-human-part-machine-is-apple-turning-us-all-into-cyborgs
12. Habitat, III. (2015). *Habitat III issues papers: 21—Smart cities*. New York. Retrieved July 8, 2020, from http://habitat3.org/wp-content/uploads/Habitat-III-Issue-Paper-21_Smart-Cities-2.0-2.pdf
13. ITU. (2020). *Joint coordination activity on internet of things and smart cities and communities (JCA-IoT and SC&C)*. Retrieved July 8, 2020, from https://www.itu.int/en/ITU-T/jca/iot/Pages/default.aspx
14. Buntz, B. (2020, February 26). In Japan, smart city projects have a social dimension. *IoT World Today*. Retrieved June 21, 2020, from https://www.iotworldtoday.com/2020/02/26/in-japan-smart-city-projects-have-a-social-dimension/

15. Forbes. (2019, December 23). Japan sparks new life in local communicates with human-centric smart cities. *Forbes*. Retrieved June 21, 2020, from https://www.forbes.com/sites/japan/2019/12/23/japan-sparks-new-life-in-local-communities-with-human-centric-smart-cities/#7d23f1a54398
16. Willis, K. S., & Aurigi, A. (2020). Introduction. In K. S. Willis & A. Aurigi (Eds.), *The Routledge companion to smart cities* (pp. 1–10). London: Routledge.
17. Merriam-Webster. (2020). *Dictionary, thesaurus*. Retrieved June 25, 2020, from https://www.merriam-webster.com/thesaurus/perceive
18. Cambridge Dictionary. (2020). UK: Cambridge University Press. Retrieved July 8, 2020, from https://dictionary.cambridge.org/dictionary/english/see?q=seeing
19. Merriam-Webster. (2020). *Dictionary, thesaurus*. Retrieved June 25, 2020, from https://www.merriam-webster.com/thesaurus/see
20. Merriam-Webster. (2020). *Dictionary, thesaurus*. Retrieved June 25, 2020, from https://www.merriam-webster.com/thesaurus/seeing
21. Merriam-Webster. (2020). *Dictionary, thesaurus*. Retrieved June 25, 2020, from https://www.merriam-webster.com/thesaurus/transparent
22. Urban Theory Lab. (2020). *Publications*. Cambridge, MA: Harvard Graduate School of Design. Retrieved July 10, 2020, from http://www.urbantheorylab.net/vision/
23. McKenna, H. P. (2021). *Visibilities and invisibilities in smart cities: Emerging research and opportunities*. Hershey, PA: IGI Global.
24. Rickert, T. (2013). *Ambient rhetoric: The attunements of rhetorical being*. Pittsburgh, PA: University of Pittsburgh Press. https://doi.org/10.2307/j.ctt5hjqwx
25. Johnson, S. B. (2006). *The ghost map: The story of London's most terrifying epidemic—And how it changed science, cities, and the modern world* (p. 236). London: Riverhead Books.
26. Lehmann, S. (2016). Sustainable urbanism: Toward a framework for quality and optimal density? *Future Cities and Environment, 2*(8), 1–29. https://doi.org/10.1186/s40984-016-0021-3
27. Nam, T., & Pardo, T. A. (2011). Smart city as urban innovation: Focusing on management, policy, and context. In E. Estevez & M. Janssen (Eds.), *Proceedings of the 5th International Conference on Theory and Practice of Electronic Governance (ICEGOV2011)* (pp. 185–194). ACM. https://doi.org/10.1145/2072069.2072100
28. Hunter, J. (2018). IoT 'conversation' and ambient contextuality. *TechCrunch*. Retrieved May 23, 2018, from https://techcrunch.com/2018/04/24/tell-me-something-good-iot-conversation-and-ambient-contextuality/
29. Mora, L., Deakin, M., Zhang, X., Batty, M., de Jong, M., Santi, P., & Appio, F. P. (2020). Assembling sustainable smart city transitions: An interdisciplinary theoretical perspective. *Journal of Urban Technology*. https://doi.org/10.1080/10630732.2020.1834831
30. Streitz, N. (2018). Beyond 'smart-only' cities: Redefining the 'smart-everything' paradigm. *Journal of Ambient Intelligence and Humanized Computing, 10*, 791–812. https://doi.org/10.1007/s12652-018-0824-1
31. Egyedi, T. M., & Mehos, D. C. (Eds.). (2012). *Inverse infrastructures: Disrupting networks from below*. Cheltenham: Edward Elgar Pub.
32. Anderson, C. (2008, June 23). The end of theory: The data deluge makes the scientific method obsolete. *Wired*. Retrieved July 1, 2020, from https://www.wired.com/2008/06/pb-theory/
33. Frenken, K., & Schor, J. (2017). Putting the sharing economy into perspective. *Environmental Innovation and Societal Transitions, 23*, 3–10.

Chapter 2
Sensing as Seeing

Creating Spaces for People in Smart Cities

2.1 Introduction

The focus of this chapter is on human sensing as a way of seeing, through the lens of the smart city [1], in real time, in the context of everyday life. As distinct from a purely technological approach to sensing as advanced through the Internet of Things (IoT) [2] and sensing as a service [3], this chapter expands upon the multi-sensorial capabilities and potentials of people as part of their "perceptive captors" and "complete sensorial apparatus" advanced by Lévy [4], from a human geography perspective. As such, the notion by McKenna [5] of complementing technological approaches to sensing with people and their sensing capabilities is further developed in this chapter.

2.2 Background

Participatory urban research projects are described by Estrin [6] in terms of people using and interacting with mobile phone technologies. Alavi, Jiao, Buttlar, and Lajnef [7] identify the need for research on challenges associated with the Internet of Things paradigm in smart cities for a range of things including "participatory sensing" where it is said that "continuing collaboration between public authorities, private companies, and academia" is required.

The exploration of sensing in this chapter gives rise to the research question, in twenty-first century cities:

Q1: Why is *sensing* as a way of seeing important for people in smart cities?

Providing additional context for this work, key terms are defined in Sect. 2.2.1.

© Springer Nature Switzerland AG 2021   17
H. P. McKenna, *Seeing Smart Cities Through a Multi-Dimensional Lens*
https://doi.org/10.1007/978-3-030-70821-4_2

2.2.1   Definitions

Definitions for key terms used in this chapter are provided for actors, agency, instrumentality, sense, sensing, and success.

Actors

Merriam-Webster Dictionary [8] defines actor as "one that acts" or "takes part in."

Agency

Merriam-Webster Dictionary [9] defines agency as "the capacity, condition, or state of acting or of exerting power." In the context of "the pedagogical and the urban" Morrison et al. [10] explore "agentive urban learning" and describe agency as "the capacity to imagine and act to create individual and collective futures."

Instrumentality

Merriam-Webster Dictionary [11] defines instrumentality as "a person or thing through which power is exerted or an end is achieved."

Sense

Merriam-Webster Dictionary [12] defines sense as "the faculty of perceiving by means of sense organs."

Sensing

McKenna [13] describes sensing as "human detection capabilities by one or more senses, as in multi-sensorial."

Success

De Haan, Haartsen, and Strijker [14] explore the defining of success in relation to the initiatives of local citizens in rural areas, finding that "as long as citizens are continuously active and in charge" initiatives are perceived to be successful.

2.3 Sensing as Spaces for People: A Theoretical Perspective

The sensing concept is explored and developed through a review of the research literature in relation to smart cities, spaces for people, agency, and emotion/affect. Key challenges are identified, and a conceptual framework is developed for sensing by people in smart cities.

2.3.1 Sensing and Smart Cities

In Guanajuato City, Mexico, researchers [15] engaged people using mobile technologies in the form of SenseCityVity, enabling youth to "observe, feel, and share" as a way to "define, document, and reflect on their city's problems." This urban mobile crowdsourcing platform experience enabled students to develop a "multimedia dataset" consisting of "geolocalized images, audio, and video" as urban data for "analysis, appropriation, and creative use" in support of community reflection and artistic creation" [15]. Quercia, Aiello, and Schifanella [16] describe efforts at "capturing the psychology of city life at scale" using "psychological maps" based on exploring the senses of people including sight, smell, hearing, and emotion. As such, using "sensory walks" Quercia et al. [16] speak in terms of "mapping the sensorial and emotional layers of cities" to "make visible what is normally not" as in, "sensory and psychological perceptions at scale" in support of future cities that are "first and foremost, about people" in "more fulfilling, humanistic, and sustainable urban environments." Konomi and Sasso [17] provide an exploration of challenges associated with "human-in-the-loop sensing" seeking to move "beyond the limitations to conventional urban sensing." Konomi and Sasso [17] highlight a range of approaches "to enable meaningful analysis of various human behaviors at scale" including in-situ sampling and meta-sensing, as in, "sensing of the urban sensing environment itself" referred to as "urban meta-sensing" and smart notifications are developed and described for in situ sampling.

With the emerging growth of Internet of Things (IoT) devices, Song, Huang, Cai, and Hong [18] claim "there are growing concerns about being sensed or monitored" using the example of cameras and microphones "in an unfamiliar house" such as an "AirBnB" thus motivating the need to "explore the design space of IoT locators to help people physically find nearby IoT devices" where locators are defined as "feedback mechanisms that can be used to physically find IoT devices." Guided by survey findings, Song et al. [18] proceeded to "design and implement low-cost locators (visual, auditory, and contextualized pictures) to help people find nearby devices." Cisco [19] on the other hand, focuses on sensor technologies in the context of a pandemic in responsive, smart cities while placing an emphasis on collaboration and partnerships.

From a sociological perspective, it is worth noting that the 2020 ISA-RC21 Conference [20] focuses on the theme of "Shaping and Sensing the City: Power,

People, Place" where RC21 refers to Research Committee 21 on Sociology of Urban and Regional Development of the International Sociological Association (ISA). Although scheduled for 2020 the conference is postponed to July 2021 due to the COVID-19 pandemic. Also of note is the October 2020 Conscious Cities Festival with an event focusing on *sensing the city* [21] and the notion that, "we read spaces." As such, the event is designed to address "how people experience space" with a view to learning more about "how it affects attitudes, behaviors, health and wellbeing." Indeed, Isin and Ruppert [22] speak of the notion of "sensory power" associated with computational technologies and the capability to track and trace people and the question of "whether the novel coronavirus pandemic has made this new form of power visible and articulable in the early 21st century."

2.3.2 Spaces for People and Smart Cities

In exploring the "design space of IoT locators, Song et al. [18] made the assumption "that people are actively taking part in finding devices" and as such, this could be said to be an example of creating spaces for people in smart cities. From a user-centered design perspective, Farkas [23] speaks in terms of the *"Language of the City* (LOTC)" as in, how people inhabit and experience the city and their appropriation through all their senses—the visual, sound, haptic, scent—for reading the text of the city. As such, according to Farkas [23], "the user of the city is in fact a *reader*" of the city. Focusing on the importance of "urban auscultation", Mattern [24] reminds us of Lefebve, in the work by Adhitya [25] and the guidance to "listen to a house, a street, a town, an an audience listens to a symphony" extended by Mattern to include "urban *systems* like transit and public health." Drawing on the theory of technological mediation and philosophical urban aesthetics, Lehtinen and Vihanninjoki [26] argue that new technologies in the form of mobile apps "enhance and add value to the everyday urban experience" in that "new digital tools increase the quality of fun when moving in familiar surroundings" and this "alters the existing environment in a way that makes more complex aesthetic qualities emerge." From their work Lehtinen and Vihanninjoki [26] suggest new hypotheses such as "efficiency alone is not a sufficient parameter to guide the design of the smart city solutions which are aimed at the use of everyday individuals" and "creative usage through the notions of fun and playfulness would significantly increase the success of implementing new solutions into the everyday."

2.3.3 Agency and Smart Cities

Historically, Angelo [27] explores "the urban as a lens" in making sense of the city, in the context of contemporary urbanization "as a way of seeing lots of things" and this "means looking not just at how city is perceived" but also, it is worth noting, "how things *other than the city* are understood through it." Haarstad and Wathne [28] present smart cities themselves as strategic actors, with "interventions to be centered on humans rather than technology" where "urban strategies around smartness are created and put in motion by strategic and pragmatic planners and other urban actors" to leverage "smart city framings to serve their own agendas and purposes." As such, Haarstad and Wathne [28] advance a "re-conceptualisation of cities—from passive receivers of smart strategies and projects to active agents assembling smartness" that "opens up many new challenges and concerns." De Waal, de Lange, and Bouw [29] describe hacking as "clever or playful appropriation of existing technologies or infrastructures" in other words "bending the logic of a particular system beyond its intended purpose or restrictions" and the 'hacker' ethos in the context of the smart city as manifesting "at individual and collective levels" that "consists of a sense of agency or 'ownership' in relation to a particular issue." In the context of the COVID-19 global pandemic, Hurley [30] speaks in terms of "design hacks" in the form of "caution tape, painted circles, plastic dividers" to name a few that "are coming from mostly nonprofessionals" in "adapting urban spaces on the fly." Design hacks are described by Hurley [30] as "attempts to rescript how people use buildings and outdoor areas during a viral pandemic" and as such, "represent the messy in-between of dealing with a crisis in real time" where "real ingenuity" emerges "under time and budget constraints." As the pandemic persists Hurley refers to how we "read the space around us for social distancing" noting that "we're always gauging our bodies in relation to our surroundings in minute detail anyway, even if we don't consciously think about it."

2.3.4 Emotion/Affect and Smart Cities

Cambria, Livingstone, and Hussain [31] propose a model for the categorization of emotion to capture affective states suitable for application in the domains of human-computer interaction (HCI), social data mining, and sentiment analysis. Paulsen, Holter Gigernes, and Koch Stigberg [32] describe the design and testing of an interactive outdoor light installation on an urban trail "controlled by sound from people's footsteps." While the installation found that the experience of color generated by people as they passed by, felt "harmonic, calming and comfortable", the prototype "did not provide a feeling of security for the whole trail" since it is "rather small" in this iteration. Raji and de Melo [33] describe an emotion analysis tool, AffectVec, for shedding light on social media-based human communication at a fine-grained level.

2.3.5 Summary

In summary, this review of the research literature highlights the importance of the human senses in smart cities, aided by the use of mobile, aware, and other technologies. Additionally, this review points to the underlying and interactive elements of human multi-sensorial capabilities as critical to human infrastructures for sensing, complementing and extending technology infrastructures of sensors, the IoT, and other emerging and aware technologies.

Table 2.1 provides an overview of the literature review by year and author in terms of challenges and opportunities. Cambria et al. [31] advance a model for the capture of affective states amenable to HCI and other aware environments.

Quercia et al. [16] address the challenge of mapping the psychology of city living at scale while looking at opportunities for the creative use of data in making cities more about people and wellbeing now and going forward. Angelo [27] advances the urban as lens for making sense of the city, for seeing the city, and for seeing through the city. Ruiz-Correa et al. [15] use an urban mobile platform experience to engage youth in a multimedia experience for thinking about city problems. Alavi et al. [7] address challenges associated with the IoT and participatory sensing calling for "continuing collaboration." Haarstad and Wathne [28] re-frame cities away from passivity to active people "assembling smartness." Konomi and Sasso [17] address the challenges of human-in-the-loop sensing through various approaches including urban meta-sensing and smart notifications for in situ sampling. De Waal et al. [29] advance hacking as playfulness appropriation of technologies or infrastructures and as a form of agency in smart cities. Cisco [19] identifies the need for sensor-driven technologies in responding to pandemic-associated

Table 2.1 Overview of the literature review for sensing as spaces for people in smart cities

Author(s)	Year	Challenges	Opportunities
Cambria et al.	2012	Emotion in aware spaces	Affective states model
Angelo	2017	Seeing in & through the city	Urban as a lens
Quercia	2017	Psychology of city living	Making cities about people
Ruiz-Correa et al.	2017		Reflection; creativity
Alavi et al.	2018	IoT and participatory sensing	
Haarstad & Wathne	2018	Reconceptualizing cities	Actors assembling smartness
Konomi & Sasso	2018	Human-in-the-loop sensing	Urban meta-sensing, etc.
de Waal et al.	2020	Appropriation of tech	Hacking as agency
Cisco	2020	Sensors for pandemics	
Farkas	2020	Appropriation by senses	LOTC
Hurley	2020	Design hacks	
Isin & Ruppert	2020	Sensory power	
Lehtinen & Vihanninjoki	2020	Everyday urban solutions	Creativity for success
Paulsen et al.	2020	Sense of security	Interaction and feeling
Raji & de Melo	2020		Emotion analysis
Song et al.	2020	Privacy	IoT device locating

	Practice / Research
Challenges	Privacy Appropriation of Technologies Human in-the-loop Sensing
Opportunities	IoT Device Location Hacking as Agency Urban Meta-sensing

Fig. 2.1 Challenges and opportunities for explorations of sensing in smart cities

challenges and opportunities in smart city environments and regions. Farkas [23] describes the *language of the city (LOTC)* as a way for people to experience and thus appropriate the city through their senses. Hurley [30] point to design hacks as rapid changes in urban environments to guide people toward safer practices in everyday spaces. Isin and Ruppert [22] propose the notion of an emergent form of power as 'sensory power,' possibly being made visible by the coronavirus pandemic. Lehtinen and Vihanninjoki [26] argue that the efficiencies afforded by technologies alone are insufficient for success and must be accompanied by creative and playful usage in smart cities. Paulsen et al. [32] explore interactive technologies in urban environments that generate a sense of comfort and harmony but not yet a sense of security. Raji and de Melo [33] explore emotion analysis at a fine-grained level using a tool for social media spaces. Song et al. [18] address challenges associated with IoTs and privacy through designing and testing locators to assist people in detecting nearby IoT devices using examples such as hotels and AirBnBs.

Viewed another way, as depicted in Fig. 2.1, challenges and opportunities for explorations of sensing in smart cities emerge for both practice and research. Challenges pertain to privacy, the appropriation of technologies, and human in-the-loop sensing, to name a few. Opportunities emerge for both practice and research in relation to IoT device location, hacking as agency, and urban meta-sensing, to name a few. This theoretical perspective provides a background and context for development, theorizing, and operationalization of a framework for sensing in smart cities and regions, as described in Sect. 2.3.6.

2.3.6 Conceptual Framework for Sensing in Smart Cities

As illustrated in Fig. 2.2, through the interactive dynamic of *people—technologies—cities*, sensing is explored though assessments of *attuning to urban spaces* in relation to emotion/affect in the form of *comfort*, as well as to *infrastructures* for *walkability* and *livability* that may be human, physical, or technological,

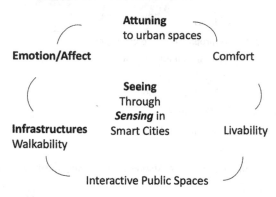

Fig. 2.2 Conceptual framework for sensing by people in smart cities

contributing to emergent *interactive public spaces* for understanding and seeing through sensing and other elements in smart urban environments and regions.

The research question posed in Sect. 2.2 is reformulated here as a proposition for exploration in this paper, as follows. In twenty-first century cities:

P1: *Sensing* as a way of *seeing* is important for people in smart cities because this enables light to be shed on experiences, assessments, and visualizations of the urban for understanding, action, and success.

2.4   Methodology

The research design for this chapter consists of an exploratory case study approach incorporating multiple methods of data collection, including survey and in-depth interviews. In support of this approach, Yin [34] points to the importance of case study research for the study of contemporary phenomena, in this case, sensing in smart cities. Sample items from Anderson's body insight scale (BIS) (2011) [35] are used in this chapter in the assessment of emotion/affect in the context of smart city environments. Where Teixiera, Dublon, and Savides [36] use a human sensing scale designed for computing technologies to detect elements such as count, identify, location, presence, and track, and where Liu, Chen, Montieri, and Pescape, [37] explore human behavior sensing as well as thing-centric approaches in addressing privacy concerns, the BIS is used here because it is intended for "assessing subtle human qualities" [38].

The process, data sources, and analysis techniques for the study underlying this chapter are described in Sects. 2.4.1–2.4.3.

2.4.1   Process

A website was used to describe the study and enable sign up, during which the gathering of basic demographic data occurred, and people could self-identify in one or more categories (e.g., educator, student, community member, city official, business, and other). Following sign up, participants were invited to complete an online survey and engage in an in-depth discussion of their experience of sensing in their city or community. The study attracted interest from individuals in cities in Canada as well as cities in northern and southern Europe, Israel, and the United States.

2.4.2   Sources of Evidence

An interview protocol and a survey instrument were developed and pre-tested prior to use in the study. In addition to questions about sensing in smart cities, the survey instrument contained a combination of closed and open-ended questions pertaining to smart cities. Additionally, a question pertaining to sensing based on the use of Anderson's body insight scale (BIS) [35] is used to explore emotion/affect in contemporary urban environments, described in more detail in Sect. 2.5.1.

In parallel with this study, evidence was systematically gathered, guided by the interview protocol, from diverse voices (e.g., city officials, business, educators, students, community members, and IT staff) in a number of Canadian cities (e.g., Toronto, Vancouver, greater Victoria) through group and individual discussions, enabling further triangulation and enriching of data.

2.4.3   Data Analysis

Content analysis was employed using a combination of deductive analysis for terminology emerging from the research literature and inductive analysis of qualitative data collected from study participants through in-depth interviews and open-ended survey questions. Descriptive statistics were used to analyze assessments of sensing data gathered from survey questions.

Overall, an analysis was conducted for n = 78 consisting of 41% females and 59% males for people ranging in age from their 20s to 70s.

2.5 Findings

Findings are presented in response to the research question, reformulated as an exploration of the proposition for sensing in terms of quantitative assessments for emotion/affect and infrastructures for walkability, livability, and interactive public spaces in smart cities. Qualitative evidence is also provided in terms of what people said about sensing in smart cities.

2.5.1 Quantitatively Assessing Sensing in Smart Cities

P1: Sensing Regarding sensing, people responded with an immediacy about their experiences in the urban environment. For example, Table 2.2 shows assessment results for sensing using *attuning to urban spaces* as a proxy. When asked to assess whether city-focused social media and other aware technologies give rise to many possibilities such as *attuning to urban spaces*, responses using a Likert-type scale with 1 = not at all and 7 = absolutely, show 50% at the upper position on the scale at 7, 33% at position 6 (sure) and 17% at position 4 (neutral).

Exploring further, when asked to assess to what extent elements such as *walkability*, *livability*, and *interactive public spaces* contribute to the making of smart cities, responses using a Likert-type scale with 1 = not at all and 7 = absolutely, are shown in Table 2.3.

Assessments for *walkability* show 17% of responses at the upper position on the scale at 7, and 50% at position 6, and 33% at position 5. Assessments for *livability* as well as for *interactive public spaces*, show 66% at position 7, 17% at position 6, and 17% at position 5.

Exploring sensing and emotion/affect responses for the sample Body Insight Scale (BIS) item,[1] pertaining to sensing in the city, the statement was posed for assessment as follows.

Table 2.2 Sensing responses: assessments of city-focused social media & aware technologies

Sensing	1	2	3	4	5	6	7
Attuning to urban spaces				17%		33%	50%

Table 2.3 Seeing responses: assessments of elements contributing to the making of smart cities

Seeing	1	2	3	4	5	6	7
Walkability					33%	50%	17%
Livability					17%	17%	66%
Interactive public spaces					17%	17%	66%

[1] "Reproduction by special permission of the Publisher, Mind Garden, Inc., www.mindgarden.com from the Body Insight Scale by Rosemarie Anderson, Ph.D. Copyright © 2011 by Rosemarie Anderson. Further Reproduction is prohibited without the Publisher's written consent."

Table 2.4 Sensing responses for city-based feelings of comfort

Sensing	1	2	3	4	5
Comfort		17%		33%	50%

Regarding your experience in your city:

1. I feel comfortable in the world most of the time

As shown in Table 2.4, on a 5-point Likert scale where 1 = strongly disagree and 5 = strongly agree, responses for feelings of comfort included 17% at position 2 (disagree), 33% at position 4, and 50% at position 5.

2.5.2 Qualitatively Speaking: What People Said about Sensing

When asked, in an open-ended survey question, "how do you sense the city?" individuals (e.g., educators, students, community leaders, community members) identified the people component, referring to, "human activity in every corner" and "the gatherings created from various festivals that often result in temporary urban interventions" and "events" that are "sociopolitical" and of a "cultural nature." A business person and educator identified "the multi layers of senses, and the feeling of dynamic." An educator made a physical and digital distinction, indicating that, "on the physical level, the number of people who are out and about on a sunny weekend, or in the evenings" and "on the digital level, keeping up-to-date with social media and online newspapers allows me to find out things my eyes could not see while walking around" adding that, "it's all part of the 'pulse of the city'." A community member in St. John's wondered whether "one's senses are more technologically aware in large cities than small" and spoke of the importance of "the visual sense of the city" that could be used by a city in "differentiating itself in a deeper way."

Indeed, when asked, "what does smartness look like in your city" a city official responded with the word, "people". A student responded that smartness looks like "nothing visible at all" adding that "on a smart device you can see a lot of wifi availability." A community member commented that "we do not see too many physical manifestations of this yet" but did indicate "I just noticed a bike counter" display on an urban mixed use trail. A community leader/member associated smart cities with "citizen-centric and inclusiveness-minded" with technology as "a tool to be mapped on top of excellent strategy, planning, approaches, and civic understanding." An educator pointed to the need "to focus on technology" in terms of "what it is for" in that a mobile urban app for example "enables people to capture evidence of their activities, actual evidence of the contribution" in order to "answer some questions, ideate about some problems in the city." However, the educator highlighted the importance of "maturity and will" on the part of city officials "to listen and understand what people want and show that they listen and understand in the form of evidence" along with "a willingness to share" and the "will and ability and the resolve to implement some of those things."

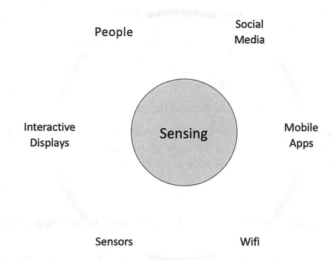

Fig. 2.3 Discussion threads for sensing by people in smart cities

Summary In summary, Fig. 2.3 provides an overview of responses to the research question in terms of discussion threads for sensing, highlighting the elements of people, social media, mobile apps, wifi, sensors, and interactive displays. Other emergent threads pertaining to sensing in smart cities suggested by Fig. 2.3 include infrastructure that may be physical, digital, or human and infrastructures that may be visible or less visible.

2.6 Discussion of Findings for Seeing as Sensing

A discussion of findings is presented in relation to assessments of *sensing* using the proxy of *attuning to urban spaces*. As shown in Table 2.2, assessments for attuning to urban spaces were strong, tending toward the upper end of the scale (e.g., 17% at the neutral position of 4, 33% at position 6, and 50% at position 7). It will be important to explore further the meaning of the 'neutral' response going forward, since according to Dourish and Bell [39] "spaces are not neutral" while Nadler, Weston and Voyles [40] point to "the use and interpretation of mid-points in items on questionnaires." Exploring sensing further through seeing, using *walkability,* as shown in Table 2.3, assessments appear somewhat strong with 17% at position 7, 50% at position 6, and 33% at position 5 on the scale. Using *livability* to explore sensing through seeing, assessments tend toward the upper end of the scale with 66% at position 7, 17% at position 6, and 17% at position 5.

People seemed to readily attune to their city in providing assessments on a sensory level for *comfort* as shown in Table 2.4 in this early-stage, exploratory glimpse of the BIS (Body Insight Scale) in the context of contemporary urban environments.

Upon further probing for comfort in the city, in-depth interviews revealed that the placement of urban elements such as benches in public spaces contributed to low comfort levels in terms of urban planning and design elements, or being a visitor to a city, in some cases, thus influencing scale rating responses. Human multi sensing capabilities in urban areas, when combined with other analytic tools and aware technologies, from smartphones to social media to urban displays with embedded sensors were understood to augment, enhance, and enrich the experience of the city, contributing to the sense of interactivity and the dynamic.

In summary, urban infrastructural elements enabling attuning to urban spaces by people may serve to support smart city success. Additionally, involving people more meaningfully in the digital and data layers of adaptive, innovative, and interactive urban elements and infrastructures involving the use of emotion/affect as sensing, may complement and enhance sensor-based supports and services contributing further to the potential for smart city success. As city officials and staff, business, community members and leaders, educators, students, and people in the city generally become more engaged with people and their sensing capabilities, the potential emerges for more aware people interacting with aware technologies in more meaningful ways, creating greater potential for success in smart cities.

2.7 Limitations, Mitigations, and Implications

A key challenge of this chapter is the small sample size involved in the underlying study and this is mitigated by in-depth interviews with diverse individuals across multiple cities. Additionally, evidence was systematically gathered from discussions with individuals and groups across sectors in parallel with this study, contributing further richness along with increased rigor from the triangulation of data. Challenges associated with elements such as geographic location and city size are further mitigated by the potential to extend this study to other cities and megaregions exceeding ten million people in size. Understanding the nature of embedded and often invisible infrastructures, whether physical (e.g., in the form of underground wires and pipes) or digital (e.g., in the form of sensors, social media spaces, and aware technologies) or human (e.g., in the form of sensing and social interactions), presented challenges that were mitigated by in-depth discussion and real world examples. The use of a proxy for assessing *sensing* such as *attuning to urban spaces* may present a limitation of this work and this is mitigated by introducing emotion/affect as an additional form of sensing through assessments for feelings of *comfort* using Anderson's [35] body insight scale (BIS).

2.7.1 Implications for Practice and Research

Going forward this work has implications for sensing in relation to practice and research in the context of smart cities and regions.

Sensing for Acting and Influencing: Implications for Practice

This chapter advances sensing by people as acting and influencing, offering pathways for urban practitioners by presenting key opportunities, as follows:

1. *Sensing and infrastructures.* Extending understandings of urban infrastructure to include human infrastructures in relation to physical and digital infrastructures incorporating notions of aware, interactive, dynamic, and adaptive and opportunities for people as meaningful actors and influencers.
2. *Sensing and urban initiatives.* Creating of urban initiatives involving people more meaningfully through their multi-sensorial capabilities as more aware people using and interacting with aware technologies, contributing to opportunities for influencing urban design, planning, and practices.

Sensing and Urban Theory and Methods: Implications for Research

This chapter evolves urban theory and approaches for researchers in identifying directions for future research, as follows:

1. *Sensing and aware people and aware technologies.* Explore and advance human multi sensorial capabilities where sensing constitutes a form of seeing by more aware people to complement and extend the technical capabilities of aware technologies (e.g., sensors, the IoT, Artificial Intelligence, and the like) in urban spaces while also serving to evolve urban theory.
2. *BIS (Body Insight Scale).* Further exploration and validation of the BIS for use in studying sensing in urban environments and regions involving more aware people interacting with each other and with aware technologies in evolving urban theory and methodologies.

In summary, key challenges and opportunities for sensing in smart cities are presented in Table 2.5 in terms of practice and research.

Additionally, implications are presented in relation to key insights, patterns, spaces for dialogue, and urban theory and methods. Key challenges for practice associated with sensing in smart cities include valuing the multi sensing capabilities of people; understanding computer sensing as an aid to people in support of, and as a complement to their multi sensing capabilities; and navigating pathways to partnering and collaborating on initiatives for sensing as seeing in the city.

Key opportunities for practice associated with sensing pertain to leveraging initiatives for the sensing of the city through people; leveraging the interplay of physical and digital infrastructures; and leveraging the people component of smartness in smart cities.

Key challenges for research associated with sensing in smart cities include the presence of neutrality responses for assessments of sensing; assessing sensing for less visible infrastructures for walkability and for interactivity; and sensing as emotion/affect. Key opportunities for research associated with sensing in smart cities

Table 2.5 Challenges, opportunities, and implications for sensing in smart cities

	Practice	Research
Challenges	Valuing multi sensing capabilities	Neutrality responses for assessments of sensing
	Computer sensing aiding multi sensing	Sensing assessments for less visible infrastructures
	Partnering/collaborating-sensing/seeing	Sensing as emotion/affect
Opportunities	Leverage sensing of city through people	What can be learned from neutral responses
	Leverage interplay of physical/digital	Sensing the invisible to generate greater awareness
	Leverage people aspect of smartness	Emotion/affect as key driver for multi sensing
Insights	Aware people and their multi sensorial capabilities in aware environments	
Patterns	Emotion/affect in urban spaces; sensing as acting and influencing by people in the city	
Spaces for dialogue	People and their multi sensing capabilities influencing urban design and planning	
Urban theory/methods	Approaches to multi sensorial capabilities in aware environments	

include the potential for learning from neutral responses to the assessment of sensing; the potential for sensing the less visible to generate greater awareness; and the potential for emotion/affect to be a key driver for human multi sensing in urban environments.

When compared with the challenges and opportunities for explorations of sensing in smart cities in Fig. 2.1 of this chapter emerging from the literature review, findings in Table 2.5 cohere with the need for: human in-the-loop sensing; collaborating and the importance of agency and people as meaningful actors; and urban meta-sensing.

In turn, a key insight from this chapter is the notion of sensing as a way of seeing in smart cities though aware people enabled by their multi sensorial capabilities in aware environments. Key patterns emerging in this chapter include the importance of emotion/affect in urban spaces; people and their sensing of visible and less visible infrastructures in urban environments; and sensing as acting and influencing by people in the city, all of which may contribute to the potential for success with smart city initiatives, endeavors, and projects. This chapter opens spaces for dialogue in relation to people and their multi sensing capabilities with the potential for influencing urban design and planning. Implications emerge for urban theory and methods associated with evolving approaches to accommodate people and their multi sensorial capabilities in aware environments.

2.8 Conclusion

This chapter uses the proxy of *attuning to urban spaces* to explore understandings of *sensing* as of way of seeing in the context of smart cities. Sensing is also explored in relation to *walkability, livability, interactive public spaces,* and *emotion/affect* in the form of feelings such as that of *comfort* in urban spaces. Focusing on sensing as a way of seeing through smart cities, this work makes a contribution to the study of sensing in the city involving the multi sensing capabilities of people. As such, urban theory is further developed and extended to include understandings of smart cities through sensing by people. Additionally, human sensory capabilities are explored through use of the BIS (Body Insight Scale) in the context of contemporary urban environments in improving quality of life with the potential of adding value to solution-making for complex urban problems. People and their multi sensorial capabilities may also serve to enrich and extend approaches to the study of smart cities. This work has implications going forward for practice, when people and their multi sensorial capabilities are taken into consideration for urban design, planning, and smart city initiatives. For research, this chapter has implications for sensing and aware people and aware technologies. Limitations of this work pertain to the small sample size and possibly the use of proxies for the exploration of *sensing* by people such as *attuning to urban spaces*. This chapter opens spaces for dialogue about people and their multi sensing capabilities with the potential for influencing urban design and planning. A key insight from this chapter is the importance of aware people enabled by their multi sensorial capabilities in aware environments. And, while writing this chapter during the COVID-19 pandemic, it is worth noting that Mattern [24] claims that during "times of crisis or change, our senses are heightened, recalibrated" suggesting that this could be a particularly poignant time for sensing the city as a way of seeing through smart cities. This work will be of interest to a broad audience including academics, students, city officials, business, community leaders, urban professionals, emotion/affect researchers, and anyone concerned with people and their multi sensorial capabilities in support of sensing as a way of seeing through smart cities and regions. As such, three questions are raised for educators, students, and community leaders, as follows:

Q 2.1. What would you say is missing from this exploration of sensing as a way of seeing through smart cities? And what would your key question or questions be?
Q 2.2. How would you describe sensing in a smart city or region?
Q 2.3. Is sensing involving spaces for people important for smart cities and regions? Please explain briefly why or why not.

If you would like to share your responses to these questions with the author of this book, an online space is provided here [https://forms.gle/KMSRiNEksK4aDXZT9].

References

1. Willis, K. S., & Aurigi, A. (2020). Introduction. In K. S. Willis & A. Aurigi (Eds.), *The Routledge companion to smart cities* (pp. 1–10). London: Routledge.
2. SCC. (2017). *Instrumentation and control.* Australia: Smart Cities Council. Retrieved December 6, 2020, from https://anz.smartcitiescouncil.com/smart-cities-information-center/instrumentation-and-control
3. Perera, C., Zaslavsky, A., Christen, P., & Georgakopoulos, D. (2014). Sensing as a service model for smart cities supported by internet of things. *Transactions on Emerging Telecommunications Technologies, 25*(1), 81–93. https://doi.org/10.1002/ett.2704
4. Lévy, J. (Ed.). (2008). *The city: Critical essays in human geography. Routledge contemporary foundations of space and place.* New York: Routledge.
5. Mckenna, H. P. (2020). Beyond confluence, integration and symbiosis: Creating more aware relationships in smart cities. In T. Ahram, W. Karwowski, A. Vergnano, F. Leali, & R. Taiar (Eds.), *Intelligent human systems integration 2020. IHSI 2020. Advances in intelligent systems and computing* (Vol. 1131). Cham: Springer. https://doi.org/10.1007/978-3-030-39512-4_161
6. Estrin, D. (2011). Participatory urban sensing. *Scientific American.* Retrieved December 26, 2016, from https://www.scientificamerican.com/citizen-science/participatory-urban-sensing-ucla/
7. Alavi, A. H., Jiao, P., Buttlar, W. G., & Lajnef, N. (2018). Internet of things-enabled smart cities: State-of-the-art and future trends. *Measurement, 129*, 589–606. https://doi.org/10.1016/j.measurement.2018.07.067
8. Merriam-Webster. (2020). *Dictionary, thesaurus.* Retrieved June 25, 2020, from https://www.merriam-webster.com/thesaurus/actors
9. Merriam-Webster. (2020). *Dictionary, thesaurus.* Retrieved June 25, 2020, from https://www.merriam-webster.com/thesaurus/agency
10. Morrison, A., Erstad, O., Liestøl, G., Pinfold, N., Snaddon, B., Hemmersan, P., & Grant-Broom, A. (2019). Investigating agentive urban learning: An assembly of situated experiences for sustainable futures. *Oxford Review of Education, 45*(2), 204–223. Special Issue on Learning Cities.
11. Merriam-Webster. (2020). *Dictionary, thesaurus.* Retrieved June 25, 2020, from https://www.merriam-webster.com/thesaurus/instrumentality
12. Merriam-Webster. (2020). *Dictionary, thesaurus.* Retrieved June 25, 2020, from https://www.merriam-webster.com/thesaurus/sense
13. McKenna, H. P. (2019). *Ambient urbanities as the intersection between the IoT and the IoP in smart cities.* Hershey, PA: IGI Global.
14. de Haan, E., Meier, S., Haartsen, T., & Strijker, D. (2018). Defining 'success' of local citizens' initiatives in maintaining public services in rural areas: A professional's perspective. *Sociologia Ruralis, 58*(2), 312–330.
15. Ruiz-Correa, S., Santani, D., Ramírez-Salazar, B., Ruiz-Correa, I., Rendón-Huerta, F. A., Olmos-Carrillo, C., ... Gatica-Perez, D. (2017). SenseCityVity: Mobile crowdsourcing, urban awareness, and collective action in Mexico. *IEEE Pervasive Computing, 16*(2), 44–53. Special issue on Smart Cities. https://doi.org/10.1109/MPRV.2017.32
16. Quercia, D., Aiello, L. M., & Schifanella, R. (2017). Mapping towards a good city life. *UD/MN Journal of Urban Design and Mental Health, 3*, 3.
17. Konomi, S., & Sasao, T. (2018). Designing a mobile behavior sampling tool for spatial analytics. In N. Streitz & S. Konomi (Eds.), *DAPI 2018, LNCS 10922* (pp. 92–100). Heidelberg: Springer. https://doi.org/10.1007/978-3-319-91131-1_7
18. Song, Y., Huang, Y., Cai, Z., & Hong, J. I. (2020). I'm all eyes and ears: Exploring effective locators for privacy awareness in IoT scenarios. *CHI 2020.* https://doi.org/10.1145/3313831.3365857
19. Cisco. (2020, April 23). In a pandemic, cities must be smarter than ever: From disinfecting robots to IoT virus sensors, new innovations can keep urban centers safe. *Government*

Technology. Retrieved August 5, 2020, from https://www.govtech.com/smart-cities/In-a-pandemic-cities-must-be-smarter-than-ever.html

20. RC21-ISA. (2020). *Conference theme*. Belgium: University of Antwerp. Retrieved August 9, 2020, from https://www.uantwerpen.be/en/conferences/rc21-sensing-the-city/conference-details/

21. CCD. (2020). *Sensing our city. Conscious cities festival*. The Centre for Conscious Design. Retrieved November 10, 2020, from https://theccd.org/event/sensing-our-city-conscious-warsaw-webinar/

22. Isin, E., & Ruppert, E. (2020, July). The birth of sensory power: How a pandemic made it visible? *Big Data & Society*. https://doi.org/10.1177/2053951720969208

23. Farkas, P. (2020). Appropriation, design and user experience in public spaces as a part of the language of the city. In A. Marcus & E. Rosenzweig (Eds.), *HCII 2020, LNCS 12202* (pp. 114–129). Cham: Springer. https://doi.org/10.1007/978-3-030-49757-6_8

24. Mattern, S. (2020, April). Urban auscultation' or, perceiving the action of the heart. *Places Journal*. Retrieved August 25, 2020, from https://placesjournal.org/article/urban-auscultation-or-perceiving-the-action-of-the-heart/

25. Adhitya, S. (2017). *Musical cities*. London: UCL Press.

26. Lehtinen, S., & Vihanninjoki, V. (2020). Seeing new in the familiar: Intensifying aesthetic engagement with the city through new location-based technologies. *Behaviour & Information Technology, 39*(6), 648–655. https://doi.org/10.1080/0144929X.2019.1677776

27. Angelo, H. (2017). From the city lens toward urbanisation as a way of seeing: Country/city binaries on an urbanising planet. *Urban Studies, 54*(1), 158–178. https://doi.org/10.1177/0042098016629312

28. Haarstad, H., & Wathne, M. W. (2018). Smart cities as strategic actors: Insights from EU Lighthouse project in Stavanger, Stockholm, and Nottingham. In A. Karvonen, F. Cugurullo, & F. Caprotti (Eds.), *Inside smart cities: Place, politics and urban innovation*. London: Routledge.

29. De Waal, M., de Lange, M., & Bouw, M. (2020). The hackable city: Exploring collaborative citymaking in a network society. In K. S. Willis & A. Aurigi (Eds.), *The Routledge companion to smart cities*. London, UK: Routledge.

30. Hurley, A. (2020, June 23). Design hacks will dominate the coronavirus recovery landscape. *Bloomberg News*. Retrieved December 20, 2020, from https://www.bloomberg.com/amp/news/articles/2020-06-23/design-hacks-will-dominate-coronavirus-recovery?__twitter_impression=true

31. Cambria, E., Livingstone, A., & Hussain, A. (2012). The hourglass of emotions. In A. Esposito et al. (Eds.), *Cognitive behavioural systems, LNCS 7403* (pp. 144–157). Berlin: Springer.

32. Paulsen, M. V., Holter Gigernes, A., & Koch Stigberg, S. (2020). Designing a new interactive outdoor light installation for a recreational urban trail. In C. Stephanidis & M. Antona (Eds.), *HCII2020, CCIS 1226* (pp. 680–684). Cham: Springer. https://doi.org/10.1007/978-3-030-50732-9_86

33. Raji, S., & de Melo, G. (2020). What sparks joy: The AffectVec emotion database. In *IW3C2 (International World Wide Web Conference Committee)*. ACM. https://doi.org/10.1145/3366423.3380068

34. Yin, R. K. (2018). *Case study research and applications: Design and methods*. Thousand Oaks, CA: Sage.

35. Anderson, R. (2011). *Body insight scale*. Retrieved July 11, 2020, from http://www.mindgarden.com/73-body-insight-scale#horizontalTab3

36. Teixiera, T., Dublon, G., & Savides, A. (2010). A survey of human sensing: Methods for detecting presence, count, location, track, and identify. *ENALAB Technical Report 09-2010, 1*(1).

37. Liu, X., Chen, H., Montieri, A., & Pescape, A. (2020). Human behavior sensing: Challenges and approaches. *Journal of Ambient Intelligence and Humanized Computing, 11*, 6043–6058. https://doi.org/10.1007/s12652-020-01861-y

38. Anderson, R. (2006). Body intelligence scale: Defining and measuring the intelligence of the body. *The Humanist Psychologist, 34*(4), 357–367.
39. Dourish, P., & Bell, G. (2011). *Divining our digital future: Mess and mythology in ubiquitous computing.* Cambridge, MA: MIT Press. https://doi.org/10.7551/mitpress/9780262015554.001.0001
40. Nadler, J. T., Weston, R., & Voyles, E. C. (2015). Stuck in the middle: The use and interpretation of mid-points in items on questionnaires. *The Journal of General Psychology, 142*(2), 71–89. https://doi.org/10.1080/00221309.2014.994590

Intelligence [...]

[...] Cambridge, Mass. [...]

[...]

Chapter 3
A Hybrid Approach to Seeing Through Smart Cities

Combining Correlational and Case Study Research Designs

3.1 Introduction

A rationale is developed in this chapter for an expansion of the methodology used so far in this book to a hybrid approach for the study of seeing through a multi-dimensional smart cities lens. As such, the exploratory case study design described in Chap. 2, involving multiple methods of data collection in the form of survey and in-depth interviews, is expanded in this chapter to include an explanatory correlational design. Yin [1] identifies the importance of a case study approach for the study of contemporary phenomena, in this case, the study of seeing through a multi-dimensional smart cities lens. However, in order to learn more about the relationships emerging from this study, an explanatory correlational design is also included. Yin [1] points to the "complementarity of case study and statistical research" adding that "case studies have been needed to examine the underlying processes that might explain a correlation." In light of the use of this hybrid approach, the conceptual framework for seeing smart cities through a multi-dimensional lens developed in Chap. 1 is revised in this chapter. Findings for explorations of sensing that emerged in Chap. 2 will be further explored in this chapter through the use of correlation, thus guiding application of the hybrid approach for the remaining chapters of this book.

3.2 Background

From the perspective of education research, Creswell [2] describes correlational research in terms of "designs to describe and measure the degree of association (or relationship) between two or more variables or sets of scores" adding that types of correlation include explanatory designs and prediction designs. Bermudez-Edo et al. [3] describe correlation coefficients as "tools to measure the dependency of two or more variables."

© Springer Nature Switzerland AG 2021
H. P. McKenna, *Seeing Smart Cities Through a Multi-Dimensional Lens*
https://doi.org/10.1007/978-3-030-70821-4_3

Providing additional context for this revised methodology, key terms used in this chapter are defined in Sect. 3.2.1.

3.2.1   Definitions

Definitions for key terms used in this chapter are provided for hybrid and correlation.

Correlation

Trochim [4] refers to a correlation as "one of the most common and most useful statistics" defining it as "a number that describes the degree of relationship between two variables."

Hybrid

Merriam-Webster Dictionary [5] defines hybrid as "produced by a combination of two or more distinct elements."

3.3   Revising the Framework for Seeing Smart Cities

The conceptual framework for seeing through smart cities, developed in Chap. 1 of this work, is revised and operationalized for use in this chapter with findings from Chap. 2, providing a guide for the chapters that follow in this book.

3.3.1   A Hybrid Conceptual Framework for Seeing in Smart Cities

As illustrated in the inner portion of Fig. 3.1, the interactive dynamic of *people—technologies—cities,* the notion of seeing smart cities is enabled through the surrounding dimensions of sensing, awareness, learning, openness, innovation, and disruption as explored in the chapters of this book, contributing to emergent understandings and findings.

An outer layer is added to this diagram to accommodate a hybrid framework for seeing through smart cities combining an exploratory case study with an

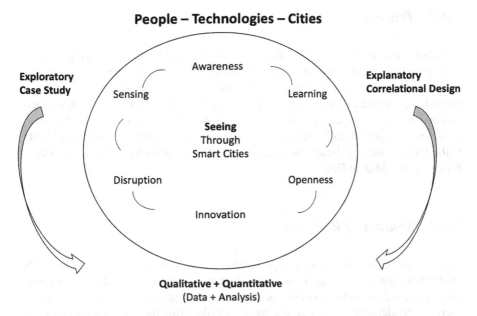

Fig. 3.1 Operationalizing the hybrid framework for seeing smart cities through a multi-dimensional lens

explanatory correlational design in support of qualitative and quantitative data collection and analysis.

3.3.2   Application of the Hybrid Framework

Application of the hybrid framework for seeing through smart cities in this chapter focuses on the sensing component that was investigated in Chap. 2 using an exploratory case study approach. This chapter applies an explanatory correlational design to the findings in Chap. 2 to enrich the qualitative data and in turn, the quantitative, correlational data is enriched through further case study analysis.

3.4   Methodology for the Hybrid Framework

The research design for this chapter included an exploratory case study approach incorporating multiple methods of data collection including survey and interview combined with an explanatory correlational design. In support of this approach, the process, data sources, and analysis techniques for the study underlying the research for this chapter are described in Sects. 3.4.1–3.4.3.

3.4.1   Process

A website was used to describe the study, enable sign up, the gathering of basic demographic data, and self-identification in one or more categories (e.g., educator, student, community member, city official, business, and other). Participants were invited to complete an online survey and through an interview engage in an in-depth discussion of their experience of smartness in their city or community. This study attracted interest from individuals, in multiple cities and multiple countries (Canada, United States, Ireland, Israel, etc.) across several continents from North America to Europe to the Middle East.

3.4.2   Sources of Evidence

A survey instrument and interview protocol were each pre-tested prior to use for the study underlying this chapter, and the latter was used to guide discussions with diverse individuals in the context of smart cities and regions about smart city spaces focusing on elements related to sensing by people, using their multi sensorial capabilities [6].

In addition to questions about smart cities, the interview protocol contains a sample question pertaining to sensing from Anderson's Body Insight Scale (2011) [7], formerly the body intelligence scale (BIS) [8], for the exploration of *comfort* in this work in contemporary urban environments, in a smart cities context. Permission from Mind Garden [7] was granted for inclusion of the comfort item in the survey instrument in order to explore feeling as sensing in the context of smart cities.

In parallel with this study, evidence was systematically gathered from diverse voices (e.g., city officials, business, educators, students, community members, and IT staff) across Canadian cities (e.g., Toronto, Vancouver, Victoria), guided by the interview protocol, enabling further triangulation and enriching of data.

3.4.3   Data Analysis

Content analysis was employed for qualitative data gathered through open-ended survey questions, interviews, and group and individual discussions using inductive analysis. This analysis was combined with deductive analysis based on terminology from the research literature. Descriptive statistics were used to analyze quantitative survey data that were gathered from questions pertaining to sensing where *attuning to urban spaces* was used as a proxy. Assessments were also analyzed for *walkability, livability,* and emotion/affect in the form of feelings of *comfort.* Using the correlation feature of the Real Statistics Resource Pack containing an add-in for Microsoft Excel [9], the Spearman correlation for ordinal data is used to explore relationships between items pertaining to sensing.

Overall, an analysis was conducted for n = 78 consisting of 41% females and 59% males for people ranging in age from their 20s to 70s.

3.5 Findings

Investigating relationships for *sensing* as a way of seeing through smart cities, findings pertaining to sensing from Chap. 2 are presented here in terms of correlations with assessments of other smart city factors. As illustrated in Table 3.1, assessments for *attuning to urban spaces* (used as a proxy for *sensing*) are correlated with assessments for *walkability*, yielding a positive Spearman correlation coefficient for ordinal data of .36.

Table 3.2 shows assessments for *attuning to urban spaces* that, when correlated with assessments for *livability*, yield a positive Spearman correlation coefficient for ordinal data of .71.

Table 3.3 shows assessments for *attuning to urban spaces* that, when correlated with assessments of feelings of *comfort*, yield a positive Spearman correlation coefficient for ordinal data of .43.

Exploring further, Table 3.4 shows assessments for *attuning to urban spaces* that, when correlated with assessments for *interactive public spaces* as being associated with smart cities, yield a positive Spearman correlation coefficient for ordinal data of .71.

Qualitatively, it is worth noting that when asked, "what do you like about being in the city?" one respondent stated, "I enjoy the scale of Victoria that contributes to its walkability" while another pointed to the importance of cities being "friendly" and "comfortable" and another stated "walking around."

Table 3.1 Assessments for attuning to urban spaces and walkability

Items	Assessments	Correlation
Attuning to urban spaces (sensing)	17% (4); 33% (6); 50% (7)	.36
Walkability	33% (5); 50% (6); 17% (7)	

Table 3.2 Attuning to urban spaces and livability

Items	Assessments	Correlation
Attuning to urban spaces	25% (5); 25% (6); 50% (7)	.71
Livability	17% (5); 17% (6); 66% (7)	

Table 3.3 Attuning to urban spaces and comfort (emotion/affect)

Items	Assessments	Correlation
Attuning to urban spaces	17% (4); 33% (6); 50% (7)	.43
Comfort	17% (2); 33% (4); 50% (5)	

Table 3.4 Attuning to urban spaces and interactive public spaces

Items	Assessments	Correlation
Attuning to urban spaces	17% (4); 33% (6); 50% (7)	.71
Interactive public spaces	17% (5); 17% (6); 66% (7)	

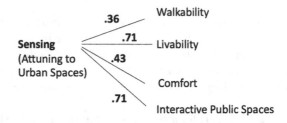

Fig. 3.2 Correlations for sensing as attuning and related factors in smart cities

3.6   Discussion: A Hybrid Approach for Seeing Through Smart Cities

In considering what can be learned from the correlations in Sect. 3.5, it is worth noting the guidance from Creswell [2] who advises that correlations in the "range from .35 to .65, are useful for limited prediction" and this would seem to be the case for *attuning to urban spaces* in relation to *walkability* with a correlation of .36 (Table 3.1) and in relation to *comfort* (emotion/affect) with a correlation of .43 (Table 3.3). However, when *attuning to urban spaces* in correlated with *livability*, a correlation of .71 emerges (Table 3.2) which, according to Creswell [2], "would be considered very good" and "good prediction can result from one variable to the other." Similarly, when *attuning to urban spaces* is correlated with *interactive public spaces* a correlation of .71 emerges (Table 3.4).

Figure 3.2 shows the correlations found between *sensing* using *attuning to urban spaces* as a proxy in relation to other factors in smart cities such as *walkability* (.36), *livability* (.71), emotion/affect in the form of feelings of *comfort* (.43), and *interactive public spaces* (.71).

Application of this explanatory correlational design for sensing serves as a model for use in the chapters that follow, on explorations of other dimensions for seeing through smart cities.

3.7   Limitations, Mitigations and Implications

As with Chap. 2, a key limitation is the small sample size in the underlying study for this chapter and this is mitigated by in-depth interviews from diverse individuals across multiple cities. The use of a proxy for *sensing* as *attuning to urban spaces* may also be a limitation of this work although this work advances *attuning to urban spaces* as a form of sensing. Another possible limitation of this chapter may be the use of the comfort item from Anderson's Body Insight Scale (BIS) [7], in the smart city context, although a promising positive correlation of .43 is found and it is worth noting that Creswell [2] advises that correlations in the .35–.65 range "are the typical values used to identify variable membership in the statistical procedure of factor analysis." Challenges associated with elements such as geographic location and city size were mitigated by the potential to extend this study to other cities and megaregions exceeding ten million people in size. Understanding the nature of pervasive, embedded and often less visible infrastructures, whether physical (e.g., in the form of underground wires and pipes and the like) or digital (e.g., in the forms of sensors, actuators, and the IoT) or human (e.g., in the form of sensing and social interactions), presented challenges that were mitigated by in-depth discussion and real world examples.

3.7.1 Implications for Practice and Research

Going forward this chapter has implications for approaches to sensing as a way of seeing through smart cities in relation to urban practice and research.

Sensing as Seeing Through Smart Cities: Implications for Practice

This work addresses challenges for practitioners in urban spaces that are associated with smart cities and regions, by presenting three key opportunities, as follows:

1. *Sensing less visible infrastructures.* Expanding understandings of urban infrastructures beyond roads and pipes and wires to include human sensing capabilities in the context of digital and data infrastructures that are aware, interactive, and adaptive.
2. *Sensing visible infrastructures.* Exploring urban initiatives involving more aware people in combination with aware technologies in relation to visible urban infrastructures in support of walkability and livability.
3. *Sensing through feelings of comfort.* Exploring and leveraging opportunities for human sensing in ways that are creative and meaningful in generating new data streams contributing to comfort in urban environments and regions.

Sensing as Seeing Through Smart Cities: Implications for Research

This work evolves smart city theory for researchers by identifying three key directions for future research, as follows:

1. *Sensing as seeing through smart cities*. Explore the leveraging of human sensory capabilities (sensing) to complement and extend the capabilities of aware technologies (e.g., sensors and the IoT), in urban spaces and regions.
2. *BIS (Body Insight Scale)*. Further exploration of the BIS for use in the context of smart cities and regions in relation to aware people and aware technologies.
3. *People and real world, real time*. Further development, exploration, and theorizing of sensing by people in smart cities focusing on real world, real time interactions, initiatives, and issues.

3.8 Conclusion

Rationale for a hybrid methodological approach to seeing through smart cities is advanced in this chapter as a way to identify relationships and learn more about the patterns for success in smart cities. The use of an exploratory case study approach in Chap. 2 is complemented in this chapter with an explanatory correlational design forming a hybrid conceptual framework for seeing through a multi-dimensional smart cities lens that is operationalized for use in this work. As such, this chapter applies an explanatory correlational design to the sensing data emerging from Chap. 2, in exploring the relationships between *sensing* (using *attuning to urban spaces* as a proxy) and other factors such as *walkability, livability, interactive public spaces*, and emotion/affect in the form of feelings of *comfort* in the city. This chapter makes a contribution to the study of smart cities in relation to people and their sensing capabilities; human multi sensorial capabilities are explored, in part, through use of a sample item from Anderson's BIS (Body Insight Scale) [7] in the context of contemporary urban environments; and sensing in the city is explored through people and their multi sensorial capabilities contributing to the notion of people as actors and more aware sensors [10, 11]. As such, this chapter highlights the importance of human sensing to keep people in-the-loop in smart cities and complements the use of sensors and the IoT (Internet of Things) [12] in addressing concerns with quality of life and the potential for greater success with solution-making in the face of complex challenges.

This work has implications going forward for (a) urban practice: in terms of opportunities for sensing less visible infrastructures; sensing visible infrastructures; and sensing through emotion/affect (e.g., feelings of comfort); and for (b) urban research: in terms of future directions for: sensing as a way of seeing through smart cities; potential for further use of the BIS (body insight scale) in the context of smart cities and regions; and meaningfully involving people as actors and influencers in real world, real time sensing.

A key relationship emerging from this chapter is that between *sensing* (using *attuning to urban spaces* as a proxy) and *livability* with a Spearman correlation coefficient of .71, said to be "very good" [2] where "good prediction can result" [2]. Another key relationship emerging from this chapter is that between *sensing* (using *attuning to urban spaces* as a proxy) and *interactive public spaces* with a Spearman correlation coefficient of .71. Also of note in relation to sensing, is the notion of less visible infrastructures that may take the form of emotion/affect (e.g., feelings of *comfort* in the city), the digital and platforms for communication between people, and mechanisms for interactivity and the sharing of information. Such less visible factors hold the potential for contributing to success in smart cities and regions. As such, a key take-away from this chapter is the critical role of people and their multi sensorial capabilities in physical and digital spaces and this will be an important consideration for practitioners and researchers in smart cities and regions. This work will be of interest to a broad audience including academics, students, city officials, business, community leaders, urban planners and designers and anyone concerned with involving people more meaningfully in sensing the city through their multi sensorial capabilities in smart cities and regions. As such, three questions are raised for educators, students, and community leaders, as follows:

Q 3.1. What would you say is missing from this approach as a way of seeing through smart cities?

Q 3.2. How would you describe the ideal approach to seeing through and understanding a smart city or region?

Q 3.3. Is it important to include both quantitative (e.g., survey) and qualitative (e.g., interview) data in an exploration of seeing through smart cities and regions? Please explain briefly why or why not.

If you would like to share your responses to these questions with the author of this book an online space is provided here [https://forms.gle/amfoxHRrDRH7DZtc9].

References

1. Yin, R. K. (2018). *Case study research and applications: Design and methods*. Thousand Oaks, CA: Sage.
2. Creswell, J. W. (2018). *Educational research: Planning, conducting, and evaluating quantitative and qualitative research* (6th ed.). Boston, MA: Pearson.
3. Bermudez-Edo, M., Barnaghi, P., & Moessner, K. (2018). Analysing real world data streams with spatio-temporal correlations: Entropy vs. Pearson correlation. *Automation in Construction, 88*, 87–100.
4. Trochim, W. M. K. (2020). *Correlation. Research methods knowledge base*. Retrieved August 10, 2020, from https://conjointly.com/kb/correlation-statistic/
5. Merriam-Webster. (2020). *Dictionary, thesaurus*. Retrieved August 10, 2020, from https://www.merriam-webster.com/dictionary/hybrid
6. Lévy, J. (Ed.). (2008). *The city: Critical essays in human geography. Routledge contemporary foundations of space and place*. New York, NY: Routledge.
7. Anderson, R. (2011). Body insight scale. *The Mind Garden Blog*. Retrieved July 11, 2020, from http://www.mindgarden.com/73-body-insight-scale#horizontalTab3
8. Anderson, R. (2006). Body intelligence scale: Defining and measuring the intelligence of the body. *The Humanist Psychologist, 34*(4), 357–367.
9. Zaiontz, C. (2020). *Real statistics using excel*. Retrieved from www.real-statistics.com

10. Resch, B. (2013). People as sensors and collective sensing—Contextual observations complementing geo-sensor network measurements. In J. M. Krisp (Ed.), *Progress in location-based services* (pp. 391–406). Berlin: Springer.
11. Sagl, G., Resch, B., & Blaschke, T. (2015). Contextual sensing: Integrating contextual information with human and technical geo-sensor information for smart cities. *Sensors, Special Issue on Sensors and Smart Cities, 15*(7), 17013–17035. https://doi.org/10.3390/s150717013
12. Du, R., Santi, P., Xiao, M., Vasilakos, A. V., & Fischione, C. (2019). The sensable city: A survey on the deployment and management for smart city monitoring. *IEEE Communications Surveys & Tutorials, 21*(2), 1533–1560. https://doi.org/10.1109/COMST.2018.2881008

Part II
Emerging Urban Patterns and Relationships Influencing and Informing Smart Cities

Chapter 4
Awareness and Seeing

People and Data in Smart Cities

4.1 Introduction

The focus of this chapter is on awareness in the city, and more particularly, in smart cities, in real time, interactive environments. For example, Ruiz-Correa et al. [1] describe urban awareness using mobile crowdsourcing in the form of SenseCityVity. Diment [2] highlights "real-time situational awareness through new data-rich technologies" pointing to the importance of collaboration and of data and the need to "integrate people, places, and processes." However, in the context of information technologies, Borning, Friedman, and Logler [3] caution that "whenever people learn something sufficiently well, they cease to be aware of it" as in "designs" for pervasive, embedded, and ubiquitous computing that "nudge toward minimizing awareness of their overall material footprint." As such, this chapter explores awareness as a dimension of seeing through smart cities, focusing on the vast and unprecedented nature of data being generated, analyzed, and processed with and through aware technologies. Challenges and opportunities for keeping people more meaningfully in-the-loop [4] are explored in support of more aware people in more sustainable and smarter cities and regions.

4.2 Background

In the United Kingdom it is said that the number of people "aware of the term 'smart cities' is less than a quarter of consumers" [5]. Yet, probing beyond the surface, to focus on "specific features" and services such as "smart utilities, smart transport, and mobility schemes" or "smart infrastructure that provides free WiFi or power" there appears to be an "appetite" if people can see "a real benefit" or if such services are "making a genuine difference to their daily lives" [5]. Halas [5] points to the

H. P. McKenna, *Seeing Smart Cities Through a Multi-Dimensional Lens*
https://doi.org/10.1007/978-3-030-70821-4_4

presence of "a huge knowledge gap" about smart cities, requiring "increased awareness" as well as "education" about the "benefits." In support of additional context
for this work, key terms are defined in Sect. 4.2.1.

4.2.1 Definitions

Definitions for key terms used in this chapter are provided for awareness and
urban data.

Awareness

Merriam-Webster Dictionary [6] defines awareness as "knowledge and understanding that something is happening or exists."

Urban Data

Tusikov [7] highlights the complexities associated with defining urban data, using
the case of Sidewalk Labs in a smart city project proposed for the city of Toronto
(and abandoned by Sidewalk Labs in mid-2020) [8]. According to Sidewalk Labs,
urban data refers to "data collected from public spaces like streets and parks" as
well as "data from publicly accessible private spaces like stores and building lobbies
or courtyards" and "data from private spaces not controlled by those who occupy
them, such as office thermostats" [7].

4.3 Awareness as Seeing: A Theoretical Perspective

Awareness as seeing in spaces for people in smart cities is explored and developed
in this chapter through a review of the research literature focusing first on awareness, people, and smart cities and then on ICTs (information and communication
technologies), urban data, and smart cities. Theoretically, this work is situated at the
intersection of socio-technical challenges and opportunities for smart cities.

4.3.1 Awareness, People, and Smart Cities

Streitz [9] speaks of social experiences in terms of awareness and connectedness in
public spaces in smart cities and risks for people associated with ICTs such as "the
loss of privacy in terms of losing control over their personal data." McKenna [10]

explores the importance of awareness in relation to people and technologies in smart cities, drawing on the work of Scharmer [11] in a conversation with Orlikowski about awareness and action and the quality of awareness. Motivated by the emerging growth of Internet of Things (IoT) devices, Song, Huang, Cai, and Hong [12] proceeded to "design and implement low-cost locators (visual, auditory, and contextualized pictures) to help people find nearby devices" as a "way of addressing a growing privacy concern about awareness of devices" in, for example, a hotel or Airbnb or other such spaces. Borning et al. [3] draw attention to embedded, cloud, and other technologies that would seem to be designed to minimize awareness of their materiality and environmental impact.

4.3.2   ICTs, Urban Data, and Smart Cities

Tusikov [7] identifies a distinction between urban data and transaction data as articulated by Sidewalk Labs where the former is said to be "anchored to geography, unlike data collected through websites and mobile phone" which constitutes the latter, although it could be argued that website and mobile phone data, if location-based, could be seen to be "anchored to geography" dynamically. Tusikov [7] states that, according to Sidewalk Labs, "data collected in physical spaces is fundamentally different from that gathered through mobile devices." According to Tusikov [7], urban data has the "defining feature" associated with "difficulty of obtaining informed consent" while "transaction data involves user consent." Yet, Tusikov [7] cautions that, even though "people have clicked the ubiquitous 'I agree' does not mean that they appreciate the terms or comprehend how their data may be used." Hudson-Smith, Hügel, and Roumpani [13] speak in terms of the mirroring of the physical world of the city in terms of the digital, as a kind of "digital twin" so that, "data can be mined, visualised, and modelled for self-monitoring, analysis and reporting" in order for the city to "respond" and "become self-aware in data terms." Hudson-Smith et al. [13] acknowledge the need for the blending of the technical "with the institutional and organizational" and "a much wider set of forces" for success. Song et al. [12] describe the use of IoT locators for other purposes than "privacy awareness" where some people appropriated the system "to learn about new IoT devices."

4.3.3   Summary

In summary, this review of the literature highlights the importance of awareness in terms of people, ICTs, and urban data in the context of smart cities. Table 4.1 provides an overview of awareness in smart cities by author and year for people, ICTs, and urban data organized by challenges and opportunities.

Table 4.1 Overview of awareness in smart cities: people, ICTs, and urban data

Author(s)	Year	Challenges	Opportunities
Scharmer	1999	Awareness, action, and quality of awareness	
Streitz	2015	Awareness	
McKenna	2016	Awareness, people and action, and IT in smart cities	
Tusikov	2019	Defining urban data	
Borning et al.	2020	Design—minimizing awareness	
Hudson-Smith et al.	2020	Collaboration	
Song et al.	2020	Device location	

Scharmer [11] argued for the importance of the quality of awareness while Streitz [9] argues that the success of smart cities depends very much on the relationship between people and technology where smart cities must be humane and sociable. McKenna (2016) [10] connects the notion by Orlikowski [11] of awareness and action with people and technologies in smart cities. Tusikov [7] highlights the defining of urban data as both a challenge and an opportunity in smart cities, while Borning et al. [3] point to the challenges associated with the design of cloud, information and communication technologies (ICTs), and other emerging technologies as contributing to the minimizing of awareness about the larger issues associated with their materiality. Hudson-Smith et al. [13] identify the challenges associated with collaboration in the use of technologies in smart cities, for self-monitoring, analysis, and reporting in real-time while Song et al. [12] explore the challenges and opportunities associated with the development of a system to assist people to become more aware with IoT device location.

Viewed another way, as depicted in Fig. 4.1, challenges emerge for both practice and research in relation to defining urban data, technologies that minimize awareness, and device location, to name a few.

Also, opportunities emerge for both practice and research in relation to defining urban data, urban data collaborations, and technology awareness, to name a few.

This theoretical perspective provides a background and context for development, theorizing, and operationalization of a framework for awareness by people in smart cities and regions.

4.3.4 Conceptual Framework for Awareness in Smart Cities

As illustrated in Fig. 4.2, through the interactive dynamic of *people—technologies—cities,* seeing as *awareness* is explored through assessments of what contributes to the making of smart cities in relation to urban data including *ICTs* and *access to public data* in relation to elements that contribute to the success of smart city projects associated factors such as *privacy* and *trust*. Options for the inclusion of other elements for assessment remain open for contributing to emergent understandings pertaining to data in urban environments and regions.

Practice / Research	
Challenges	Defining urban data
	Technologies that minimize awareness
	Device location
Opportunities	Defining urban data
	Urban data collaborations
	Technology awareness

Fig. 4.1   Challenges and opportunities for explorations of awareness in smart cities

Fig. 4.2   Conceptual framework for awareness by people in smart cities

This exploration of awareness in relation to urban data in smart city environments gives rise to the research question, in twenty-first century cities:

Q1: Why is *awareness* important in relation to the generation of data in smart cities?
   The research question is reformulated here as a proposition for exploration in this chapter, as follows.

P1: *Awareness* is important in relation to the generation of data in smart cities in many ways, on many levels, including the use of information and communication technologies (ICTs) and associated issues of privacy and trust.

4.4   Methodology

The research design for this work includes an exploratory case study approach incorporating multiple methods of data collection (e.g., survey and in-depth interviews) combined with an explanatory correlational design. In support of this approach, this work is attentive to Yin [14] who points to the importance of case study research for the study of contemporary phenomena, in this case, awareness in smart cities. This work is also attentive to Creswell [15] who describes correlational research in terms of "designs to describe and measure the degree of association (or relationship) between two or more variables or sets of scores." The process, data sources, and analysis techniques for the study underlying the research for this chapter are described in Sects. 4.4.1–4.4.3.

4.4.1 Process

A website was used to describe the study, enable sign up, the gathering of basic demographic data, and self-identification in one or more categories (e.g., educator, student, community member, city official, business, and other). Participants were invited to complete an online survey and engage in an in-depth discussion of their experience of awareness in their city or community. The study attracted interest from individuals in countries in North America (e.g., Canada and the United States) extending to countries in Europe (e.g., Greece, Ireland, etc.), and the Middle East (e.g., Israel).

4.4.2 Sources of Evidence

A survey instrument with open-ended and closed questions and an interview protocol were developed and pre-tested prior to use in the study focusing on questions pertaining to smart cities.

In parallel with this study, evidence was systematically gathered through individual and group discussions from diverse voices (e.g., city officials, business, educators, students, community members, and IT staff) across Canadian cities (e.g., Toronto, Vancouver, Victoria) enabling further triangulation and enriching of data.

4.4.3 Data Analysis

Descriptive statistics were used in the analysis of survey data while content analysis was employed for open ended survey question data and interview data. Content analysis was used in the analysis of qualitative data through a combination of deductive analysis on terminology from the research literature and inductive on data collected from study participants. Using the correlation feature of the Real Statistics Resource Pack containing an add-in for Microsoft Excel [16], correlations were conducted on descriptive statistics to determine the Spearman correlation coefficients for ordinal data from assessments of awareness, ICTs, and other variables.

In parallel with this study data were also analyzed systematically from individual and group discussions across many sectors in several Canadian cities (e.g., Toronto, Vancouver, and Victoria). Overall, an analysis was conducted for n = 78 consisting of 41% females and 59% males for people ranging in age from their 20s to 70s.

4.5 Findings

Findings are presented in response to the research question based on the proposition in terms of explorations of *awareness, ICTs, access to public data, privacy* and *trust*. For assessments of awareness as an element contributing to the making of smart cities, on a seven point Likert scale with 1 = Not at all and 7 = Absolutely, Table 4.2 shows responses tending toward the upper end of the scale with 25% at position 5, 25% at position 6, and 50% at position 7.

For assessments of ICTs as an element contributing to the making of smart cities, on a seven-point Likert scale with 1 = Not at all and 7 = Absolutely, Table 4.3 shows responses also tending toward the upper end of the scale with 50% at position 5 and 50% at position 7.

Using the Real Statistics add-in for Microsoft Excel [16], Table 4.4 shows assessments for *awareness* that, when correlated with assessments for *ICTs*, yields a Spearman correlation coefficient for ordinal data of −.23.

Exploring further, Table 4.5 shows assessments for *awareness* that, when correlated with responses for assessments of *access to public data*, yields a Spearman correlation coefficient for ordinal data of .23.

Table 4.2 Awareness responses assessed for contributing to the making of smart cities

Items	1	2	3	4	5	6	7
Awareness					25%	25%	50%

Table 4.3 ICT responses assessed as an element contributing to the making of smart cities

Items	1	2	3	4	5	6	7
ICTs					50%		50%

Table 4.4 Assessments for awareness and ICTs

Items	Assessments	Correlation
Awareness	25% (5); 25% (6); 50% (7)	−.23
ICTs	50% (5); 50% (7)	

Table 4.5 Assessments for awareness and access to public data

Items	Assessments	Correlation
Awareness	25% (5); 25% (6); 50% (7)	.23
Access to public data	50% (6); 50% (7)	

Table 4.6 Assessments for awareness and trust

Items	Assessments	Correlation
Awareness	25% (5); 25% (6); 50% (7)	−.54
Trust	25% (6); 75% (7)	

Table 4.7 Assessments for awareness and privacy

Items	Assessments	Correlation
Awareness	25% (5); 25% (6); 50% (7)	−.23
Privacy	50% (6); 50% (7)	

Table 4.8 Assessments for ICTs and trust

Items	Assessments	Correlation
ICTs	50% (5); 50% (7)	.57
Trust	25% (6); 75% (7)	

Table 4.9 Assessments for ICTs and privacy

Items	Assessments	Correlation
ICTs	50% (5); 50% (7)	.57
Privacy	50% (6); 50% (7)	

Exploring further, Table 4.6 shows assessments for *awareness* that, when correlated with responses for assessments of *trust* as contributing to increased value for data in smart cities, yields a Spearman correlation coefficient for ordinal data of −.54.

Exploring further, Table 4.7 shows assessments for *awareness* that, when correlated with responses for assessments of *privacy* as contributing to increased value for data in smart cities, yields a Spearman correlation coefficient for ordinal data of −.23.

On the other hand, exploring further, Table 4.8 shows assessments for *ICTs* that, when correlated with responses for assessments of *trust* as contributing to increased value for data in smart cities, yields a Spearman correlation coefficient for ordinal data of .57.

Exploring further, Table 4.9 shows assessments for *ICTs* that, when correlated with responses for assessments of *privacy* as contributing to increased value for data in smart cities, yields a Spearman correlation coefficient for ordinal data of .57.

When asked how people are becoming more aware of smart cities and smart technologies:

- 67% indicated that people generally are not aware of smart cities;
- 67% indicated that city initiatives are really helping to generate smart city awareness;

- 83% indicated that education programs in schools and universities are helping to generate smart city awareness; and to a lesser extent at
- 33%, smart cities awareness is occurring through the media.

Qualitatively, a glimpse of what people said is provided based on open-ended survey questions, in-depth interviews, and individual and group discussions. Indeed, one individual responded that "being aware" of being a "citizen of the city" contributes to the making of a smart city. Of note in a data context is an observation by an urban educator that students are "not interested in the archive, the data management, in holding on to things" highlighting questions such as—"what does it look like when we connect with each other" in the moment. When asked how social media and other aware technologies are affecting your experience of the city, a community leader responded that they "assist in citizen/visitor education and awareness" adding that "unfortunately, most cities are not utilizing them in this manner." Another community leader/member identified the need to educate people about smart cities and figure out how to "visualize this data" and "how to make it about more than data" in order "for the general public to be interested and understand more."

4.6   Discussion of Awareness: People and Data in Smart Cities

Creswell [15] advises that for correlations in the "range from .20 to .35, there is only a slight relationship" and this would seem to be the case for *awareness* when correlated with *ICTs*, however what emerges is a negative, inverse correlation of −.23. When *awareness* is correlated with *access to public data*, a positive Spearman correlation for ordinal data of .23 emerges, again suggestive of only a "slight relationship" [15]. Yin [14] claims that "case studies have been needed to examine the underlying processes that might explain a correlation" and it is here where additional responses from interviews and open-ended survey questions, and group and individual discussions may assist. The inverse and "slight relationship" (−.23) found between awareness and ICTs in this chapter is interesting in light of the response by one individual that "most cities are not utilizing" social media and other aware technologies in ways that contribute to citizen education and awareness. This commentary also serves possibly to shed light on the positive "slight relationship" (.23) that emerged between *ICTs* and *access to public data*. Also, the claim by Borning et al. [3] that "the materiality of information technology is largely invisible" is important because it may also assist in explaining or shedding light on the inverse, negative and slight relationship between awareness and ICTs and the inverse relationships between *awareness* and *trust* (−.54) and *awareness* and *privacy* (−.23).

Correlations between *ICTs* and *privacy* (.57) and *ICTs* and *trust* (.57) are also noteworthy, in that Creswell [15] advises that correlations in the range from .35 to .65, "are useful for limited prediction."

Figure 4.3 shows the correlations found between *awareness* and other factors in smart cities such as *ICTs* and *access to public data*. as well as *privacy* and *trust*. Correlations between *ICTs* and *privacy* and *trust* are also shown here.

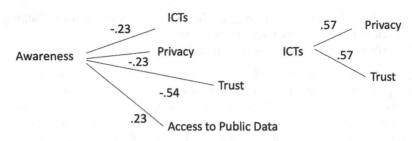

Fig. 4.3 Correlations for awareness and related factors in smart cities

The need for more education about data and what it means, identified by one respondent would seem to support the need identified by Halas [5] for more education to address gaps in knowledge. This, along with the need for finding ways to more meaningfully "visualize this data" may assist in shedding light on the "slight relationship" found between *awareness* and *access to public data*. Education programs are credited with contributing to an awareness of smart cities by survey respondents (88%) even though findings in this work suggest that people are generally not aware of smart cities (67%) and that city initiatives are important for generating awareness of smart cities (67%) with media playing a lesser role (33%) of informing about smart cities.

4.7   Limitations, Mitigations, and Future Implications

A key challenge of the findings in this chapter is the small sample size and this was mitigated by in-depth interviews with diverse individuals across multiple cities in multiple countries. Additionally, evidence systematically gathered in parallel with this study, contributed further richness along with increased rigor from the triangulation of data. Challenges associated with elements such as geographic location and city size are mitigated by the potential to extend this study to other cities and mega-regions exceeding ten million people in size. Challenges associated with the intangible nature of awareness in smart cities are mitigated by in-depth discussion and real world examples.

4.7.1   Implications for Practice and Research

Going forward, findings in this chapter have implications for practice and research in the context of smart cities and regions.

Awareness and Smart Cities: Implications for Practice

This work highlights awareness by people in relation to aware technologies (in the form of ICTs) and access to public data, identifying pathways for urban practitioners in smart cities by presenting three key opportunities, as follows:

1. *Urban data awareness.* Expanding understandings of urban data through data visualizations
2. *Awareness of aware technologies.* Expanding technology and urban data awareness through involving people in education opportunities and initiatives.
3. *Awareness as seeing.* Providing increased opportunities in educating people about the importance of privacy and trust and awareness as seeing in smart cities.

Awareness and Smart Cities: Implications for Research

This chapter contributes to the evolving of urban theory and methodological approaches for researchers in relation to awareness and smart cities by identifying directions for future research, as follows:

1. *Awareness of public data and potentials.* Further exploration of the awareness of access to public data and associated potentials for enhancing the experience of urban spaces in contributing to the success of smart city initiatives and solutions.
2. *Awareness as seeing the less visible.* Further development and exploration of becoming more aware of the less visible aspects of smart cities and regions associated with data generation, processing, and analysis.
3. *Awareness: people, data, and technologies.* Further development, exploration, and theorizing of awareness focusing on the dynamic of people, data, and technologies in relation to real world, real time interactions, initiatives, and issues associated with privacy and trust in smart cities and regions.

In summary, based on findings in this chapter, challenges and opportunities for explorations of awareness in smart cities are presented in Table 4.10 in terms of practice and research. Challenges for practice include visualizing urban data; educating people to increase awareness about smart cities; and the importance of privacy and trust in support of education and awareness as seeing in smart cities.

Challenges for research include understanding urban data; understanding awareness in smart cities; and understanding access to public data. Opportunities for practice include leveraging awareness in the city through people; leveraging technologies to assist people in becoming more aware of technologies; and leveraging the people component of ICTs. Opportunities for research include becoming aware of potential uses for public data; becoming more aware of the less visible in smart cities; and understanding access to public data.

Additionally, Table 4.10 highlights key insights associated with the nature of the relationship between awareness and ICTs in smart cities, inverse as it is at −.23. Patterns in this chapter pertain to issues associated with ICTs, privacy, trust, access

Table 4.10 Challenges & opportunities for explorations of awareness in smart cities

	Practice	Research
Challenges	Visualizing urban data	Understanding urban data
	Educating to increase awareness about SCs	Understanding awareness in smart cities
	Privacy and trust—awareness as seeing	Understanding access to public data
Opportunities	Leveraging awareness the city by people	Becoming aware of potential uses for public data
	Leveraging tech to become aware of tech	Becoming more aware of the less visible in cities
	Leveraging the people component of ICTs	Understanding access to public data

Insights	The nature of the relationship between awareness & ICTs in smart cities as inverse (−.23)
Patterns	Issues associated with ICTs, privacy, trust & access to public data in relation to awareness
Spaces for dialogue	People and their awareness of ICTs & data, influencing urban design and planning
Urban theory methods	Approaches to and awareness of people in aware technology environments

to public data in relation to awareness while spaces for dialogue are highlighted as people and their awareness of ICTs and data, influencing smart city initiatives for urban design and planning. Urban theory and methods are highlighted in terms of the importance of the awareness dimension of people in aware technology environments.

It is worth noting that when compared with the challenges and opportunities for explorations of awareness in smart cities in Fig. 4.1 of this chapter emerging from the literature review, findings in this chapter highlighted in Table 4.10 cohere with the need for: further defining and understanding urban data; collaborating around not just urban data but educating for awareness of data; and educating for greater technology awareness.

4.8 Conclusion

This chapter explores awareness as a way of seeing through smart cities and regions. Focusing on the smart city elements of *ICTs* (information and communication technologies) and *access to public data,* this work makes a contribution to the study of seeing through smart cities as follows: first, awareness as an approach to the study of urban spaces is further developed and extended to include a conceptualization framework for awareness involving people in smart cities; second, smart city theory is further developed with the addition of awareness theorizing; and third, people and their awareness of urban data and access to public data is explored. This work has implications going forward for: (a) practice, making recommendations related to: urban data awareness, awareness of aware technologies, and awareness as seeing and (b) research, making recommendations related to: awareness of public data and potentials; awareness as seeing the less visible; and awareness and the people, data, and technologies dynamic. A key takeaway from this work is the nature of the relationship between *awareness* and *ICTs* in smart cities, found to be a slight, inverse one with a Spearman correlation for ordinal data of −.23. However, when *awareness* is correlated with *access to public data* a slight relationship is found with a positive Spearman correlation coefficient of .23 with implications possibly for improving possibilities for smart city success in support of work by Hudson-Smith et al. [13]. Further, the correlation between *ICTs* and *trust* reveals a positive and stronger relationships at .57 as people become more aware of ICTs and of the value of data. A key limitation of this work is the small sample size while opening spaces for dialogue around people and their awareness of ICTs and data with the potential for influencing smart city initiatives and urban planning and design. This work will be of interest to a broad audience including academics, students, city officials, business, community leaders, urban professionals and anyone concerned with awareness in support of seeing and understanding smart cities and regions. As such, three questions are raised for educators, students, and community leaders, as follows:

Q 4.1. What would you say is missing from this exploration of awareness as a way of seeing through smart cities? And what would your key question or questions be?

Q 4.2. How would you describe awareness in a smart city or region?

Q 4.3. Is awareness in relation to people and data important for smart cities and regions? Please explain briefly why or why not.

If you would like to share your responses to these questions with the author of this book an online space is provided here [https://forms.gle/ZfvX5kBQhN93cwPf7].

References

1. Ruiz-Correa, S., Santani, D., Ramírez-Salazar, B., Ruiz-Correa, I., Rendón-Huerta, F. A., Olmos-Carrillo, C., ... Gatica-Perez, D. (2017). SenseCityVity: Mobile crowdsourcing, urban awareness, and collective action in Mexico. *IEEE Pervasive Computing, 16*(2), 44–53. Special issue on Smart Cities. https://doi.org/10.1109/MPRV.2017.32
2. Diment, R. (2020, February 15). Are smart cities actually safer? *Smart City Dive*. Retrieved August 15, 2020, from https://www.smartcitiesdive.com/news/are-smart-cities-actually-safer/572861/
3. Borning, A., Friedman, B., & Logler, N. (2020). The 'invisible' materiality of information technology. *Communications of the ACM, 63*(6), 57–64.
4. Streitz, N. (2018). Beyond 'smart-only' cities: Redefining the 'smart-everything' paradigm. *Journal of Ambient Intelligence and Humanized Computing, 10*, 791–812. https://doi.org/10.1007/s12652-018-0824-1

5. Halas, N. (2018, December 13). How well do we really understand smart cities? *IoT For All.* Retrieved August 15, 2020, from https://www.iotforall.com/smart-city-research/
6. Merriam-Webster. (2020). *Dictionary, thesaurus.* Retrieved August 16, 2020, from https://www.merriam-webster.com/dictionary/awareness
7. Tusikov, N. (2019, August 6). "Urban data" & "civic data trusts" in the smart city. *Ryerson University, Centre for Free Expression, Blog.* Retrieved August 18, 2020, from https://cfe.ryerson.ca/blog/2019/08/"urban-data"-"civic-data-trusts"-smart-city
8. Smart Cities World. (2020, May 11). Sidewalk labs shuts down Toronto smart city project. *News.* Retrieved August 19, 2020, from https://www.smartcitiesworld.net/news/news/sidewalk-labs-shuts-down-toronto-smart-city-project-5262
9. Streitz, N. A. (2015). Citizen-centered design for humane and sociable hybrid cities (keynote address). In *Proceedings of Third International Biannual Conference—Hybrid City 2015—Data to the People, University of Athens, Greece.*
10. McKenna, H. P. (2016). Is it all about awareness? People, smart cities 3.0, and evolving spaces for IT. In *Proceedings of SIGMIS-CPR'16* (pp. 47–56). Alexandria, VA: ACM. https://doi.org/10.1145/2890602.2890612
11. Scharmer, C. O. (1999). *Awareness is the first and critical thing: Conversation with Professor Wanda Orlikowski.* Cambridge, MA: MIT, Sloan School of Management.
12. Song, Y., Huang, Y., Cai, Z., & Hong, J. I. (2020). I'm all eyes and ears: Exploring effective locators for privacy awareness in IoT scenarios. *CHI 2020.* https://doi.org/10.1145/3313831.3365857
13. Hudson-Smith, A., Hügel, S., & Roumpani, F. (2020). Self-monitoring, analysis and reporting technologies: Smart cities and real-time data. In K. S. Willis & A. Aurigi (Eds.), *The Routledge companion to smart cities.* London: Routledge.
14. Yin, R. K. (2018). *Case study research and applications: Design and methods.* Thousand Oaks, CA: Sage.
15. Creswell, J. W. (2018). *Educational research: Planning, conducting, and evaluating quantitative and qualitative research* (6th ed.). Boston, MA: Pearson.
16. Zaiontz, C. (2020). *Real statistics using excel.* Retrieved from www.real-statistics.com

Chapter 5
Learning and Data in Smart Cities

5.1 Introduction

This chapter focuses on learning as a lens for understanding and seeing through smart cities. An exploration of the research and practice literature for learning cities [1] is conducted, attentive to the challenges and opportunities associated with community engagement, participation, and equity [2] as well as privacy and trust [3] generally, and in relation to data [4] in smart environments. Using an exploratory case study approach combined with an explanatory correlational design, *community participation* as a proxy for *learning* is explored in relation to data, focusing on people and their experiences and assessments in smart cities pertaining to *privacy*, *security*, *trust*, interactive displays, and data visualizations.

5.2 Background

Nam and Pardo [1] identified learning city as a fundamental component of smart cities, where, focusing on the human dimension, creativity is said to be "a key driver to smart city, and thus people, education, learning, and knowledge have central importance." The concept of "smart people" is also described by Nam and Pardo [1], encompassing factors such as "affinity to life long learning, social and ethnic plurality, flexibility, creativity, cosmopolitanism or open-mindedness, and participation in public life." Ferronato and Ruecker [2] speak in terms of "smart citizenship" for more sustainable and inclusive smart cities.

Providing additional context for this work, key terms are defined in Sect. 5.2.1.

© Springer Nature Switzerland AG 2021
H. P. McKenna, *Seeing Smart Cities Through a Multi-Dimensional Lens*
https://doi.org/10.1007/978-3-030-70821-4_5

5.2.1   Definitions

Definitions for key terms used in this work are provided based on the practice and research literature for data, privacy, security, trust, and learning cities.

Data

The Merriam-Webster Dictionary [5] defines data as "information in digital form that can be transmitted or processed" and as "information output by a sensing device or organ that includes both useful and irrelevant or redundant information and must be processed to be meaningful."

Privacy

The Merriam-Webster Dictionary [6] defines privacy as "freedom from unauthorized intrusion."

Security

The Merriam-Webster Dictionary [7] defines security as "freedom from danger" and as "freedom from fear and anxiety."

Trust

The Merriam-Webster Dictionary [8] defines trust as "assured reliance on the character, ability, strength, or truth of someone or something."

Learning Cities

UNESCO [9] describes a learning city as one that "effectively mobilizes its resources in every sector to promote inclusive learning from basic to higher education" with attention to "learning in families and communities" as well as "the workplace" along with "modern learning technologies" and "quality and excellence in learning" advancing "a culture of learning throughout life" and as such "promotes lifelong learning for all" as "a foundation for sustainable social, economic, and environmental development."

5.3 Learning and Data in Smart Cities: A Theoretical Perspective

The learning concept is explored and developed through a review of the research literature for smart cities and learning cities. Focus is placed on learning and smart cities and then data and smart cities. Challenges and opportunities for learning and data in smart cities are also explored.

5.3.1 Learning and Smart Cities

Borgman et al. [10] provided a report on knowledge infrastructures "to support new ways of thinking and acting" in response to rapid change "around us" regarding "how people create, share, and dispute knowledge." Borgman et al. [11] revisit this work again more recently finding that "such infrastructures are increasingly fragile, and often brittle, in the face of open data and open source, the demise of gatekeepers, and shifting public and private boundaries that redistribute power." From the perspective of lifelong and lifewide learning, Zhuang, Fang, Zhang, Lu, and Huang [12] claim that "learning environments have expanded from schools to the whole city" including "school, family, community, workplace, and museum as typical learning environments in a smart city." Ferronato and Ruecker [2] describe "smart citizenship" as occurring "when people become active stakeholders, engaged in long term relationships in the process of planning, developing, testing, implementing, and evaluating urban decisions, actions, and policies." As such, for Ferronato and Ruecker [2] the notion of "smartness" pertains to "the use of technology" and also to "participation and engagement" where the focus is placed on open design practices and meta-design as "an emerging design culture" creating spaces for new forms of interaction. Facer and Buchczyk [13] identify the need "to understand the learning infrastructure of a city" in terms of "the city streets, parks, and transport systems" as well as "schools, colleges, and universities." In another article in the special issue on learning cities, Facer and Buchczyk [14] argue that this learning infrastructure "is made of people, personal relations, and emotion as much as funding and material resources" and as such, is characterized by fragility and dynamism. Lido, Reid, and Osborne [15] present findings from a case study of informal learning and lifewide literacies using "novel data strands" such as "GPS trails that track mobility around the city" along with "the naturally occurring social media" while seeking to "offer the capacity to build citizens' agency through literacy practices and less formal learning opportunities."

Manchester and Cope [16] address the issue of how "to include citizens in smart city development" proposing a "creative citizens model" using the example of Created By Us Damp Busters project. The project [16] shows "how practices of situated, critical learning might be adopted with citizens on a Smart City project" while "accounting for the everyday lives and unequal relations of power, knowledge and resources in the area." The project [16] also shows "the need to provide multiple and varied opportunities for participation; and direct engagement in building technologies together" while "making visible technology design processes" and "ethical issues" among other benefits. Lister [17] speaks in terms of "smart learning" in communities in mediating and "supporting digital skills and literacies" for people, framed as "autonomous smart learning journeys" using "a digital skills framework" together with "a pedagogy of experience complexity." Two categories within the experience complexity for a smart learning journey involve seeing. For example, the "being there" category involves "seeing the whole and related parts" while the "knowledge & place as value" category involves "seeing knowledge and place as valuable." Chauncey and Simpson [18] highlight the importance of a participatory approach to visioning and other activities in advancing the notion of learning city 'smart teams' in relation to "promoting, supporting and extending the community school model." Smart teams are proposed in addressing "systemic and structural inequities and disparities in social, health, economic, and educational opportunities" [18] drawing on self-determination theory, communities of networked expertise, and activity theory.

5.3.2 Data and Smart Cities

From a government technology perspective, Castro [19] refers to learning cities as "networks of smart cities that allow for government agencies to exchange metrics and discover data-driven insights not only from within their own communities but also from their peers in other locales." McKenna [20] advanced the notion of data as ambient in smart cities and ways of increasing literacies in smart cities (2019) [21]. Weber [22] points to the need for cities to become more "inhabitant-centric" as in, "pay more attention to the people who live in them." Manchester and Cope [16] identify concerns by citizens with issues of data privacy making reference to the Facebook data scandal associated with Cambridge Analytica. Currie [23] explores the performative nature of data when used by cities for "impression management" with real time data visualizations that may portray "city administration as competent, trustworthy, and open to citizen feedback" while not having allowed for real citizen engagement "from a place of contestation about what societal issues are most pressing and how to frame them." Tavmen [4] advances the concept of 'data/ infrastructure' where, using the example of Citymapper, "users become infrastructure" in "fixing and creating data" associated with transport, and as such, extends to 'fixing infrastructure" playing out in "everyday socio-technical and socio-spatial modulations" thus involving people meaningfully in the functioning of the app and "the app's successful development."

Ismagilova et al. [3] provide a review of the research literature for privacy and security in smart cities including a section on trust challenges while acknowledging limitations of their work associated with the lack of "human-centred factors" from the "citizen perspective". Sophus Lai and Flensburg [24] advance the notion of "a proxy for privacy" through an exploration of "the surveillance ecology of mobile apps." In response to the "ubiquitous maps and graphs of COVID-19", the global pandemic, Bowe, Simmons, and Mattern [25] identify collaborations between "artists, designers, data scientists, and public health officials" where data visualizations are being generated "about local dynamics and neighborhood mutual aid networks and personal geographies of mitigation and care" to fill knowledge gaps and "encourage critical thinking about how COVID-19 data is sourced and modeled."

5.3.3 Summary

In summary, this review of the literature highlights the importance of learning for smart cities as shown in Table 5.1, by author and year in terms of challenges and opportunities. Borgman et al. [11] address the need for rethinking knowledge infrastructures in the context of massive transformations while considering what had been learned and future directions [12]. Castro [19] highlights cities as networks enabling data driven insights, with challenges and opportunities. McKenna [20] advances the notion of ambient data in the public realm in smart cities and the need for data literacies in smart environments [21]. Ferronato and Ruecker [2] advance the notion of "open (meta) design practices" in support of smart citizenship. Facer and Buchczyk [13, 14] use the example of walking in the city to demonstrate the challenges and opportunities associated with learning infrastructures. Lido et al.

Table 5.1 Overview of learning and data in smart cities as challenges and opportunities

Author(s)	Year	Challenges	Opportunities
Borgman et al.	2013	Knowledge infrastructures	
Castro	2017	Cities as networks; Data driven insights	
McKenna	2017	Ambient data	
Ferronato & Ruecker	2018	Meta-design for interaction, engagement, participation	
Facer & Buchczyk	2019	Learning infrastructures	
Lido et al.	2019	Informal learning; Lifewide literacies	
Manchester & Cope	2019		Creative citizens model
McKenna	2019	Data and access	
Weber	2019	Inhabitant-centric	
Borgman et al.	2020	Knowledge infrastructures	
Bowe et al.	2020	Counter-mapping the COVID-19 pandemic data	
Chauncey & Simpson	2020	Learning city smart teams—participatory approach	
Currie	2020	Citizen engagement; Trust	Data as performance
Ismagilova et al.	2020	Privacy, security, trust	
Lister	2020	Smart learning journeys—digital skills & literacies	
Sophus Lai & Flensburg	2020	Proxy for privacy and mobile apps	
Tavmen	2020	Data/infrastructure	
Zhuang et al.	2020	Lifelong & lifewide learning	

[15] focus on informal learning and lifewide literacies as challenges and opportunities for smart cities. Manchester and Cope [16] explore models for learning in city contexts, advancing the opportunity for a creative citizens model.

McKenna [21] explores the challenges and opportunities of data and access in terms of literacies in smart cities. Weber [22] advances the need for cities to become more inhabitant-centric while Bowe et al. [25] involve people across sectors in counter-mapping interventions to show through data visualizations what is occurring locally, and Chauncey and Simpson [18] describe a participatory approach to learning cities using smart teams to address systemic and structural inequities and disparities. Currie [23] frames data as performance in smart cities while highlighting the importance of citizen engagement and trust.

Ismagilova et al. [3] address largely technological issues associated with privacy and security in smart cities while noting the importance of trust in relation to people. Lister [17] articulates the notion of smart learning journeys in support of digital skills and literacies in communities. Sophus Lai and Flensburg [24] explore big data issues through an exploration of smartphone privacy and mobile apps. Tavmen [4] explores data-driven and platform urbanism using Citymapper while highlighting the participation of people in the data-driven city. Zhuang et al. [12] focus on the challenges of lifelong learning in smart cities in addition to lifewide learning.

Viewed another way, as depicted in Fig. 5.1, challenges emerge for both practice and research in relation to learning in technology embedded environments.

Challenges pertain to defining urban learning; learning infrastructures; and people and their data interactions. Opportunities emerge for both practice and research in relation to: lifewide and lifelong literacies; learning infrastructures; and data literacies, to name a few.

Additionally, this review points to the underlying and interactive element of data as critical to human infrastructure for learning, complementing and extending physical infrastructures.

	Practice / Research
Challenges	Defining urban learning
	Learning infrastructures
	People and data interactions
Opportunities	Lifewide and lifelong literacies
	Learning infrastructures
	Data literacies

Fig. 5.1 Challenges and opportunities for learning and data in smart cities

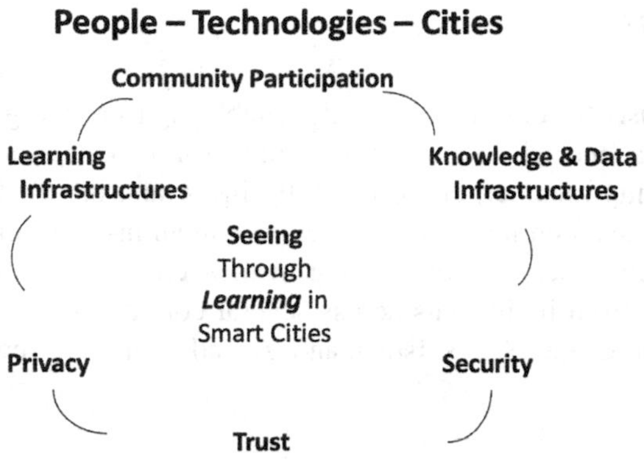

People – Technologies – Cities

Community Participation

Learning
Infrastructures

Knowledge & Data
Infrastructures

Seeing
Through
Learning in
Smart Cities

Privacy

Security

Trust

Fig. 5.2 Conceptual framework for learning and data in smart cities

5.3.4 Conceptual Framework for Learning and Data in Smart Cities

This theoretical perspective provides a background and context for development, theorizing, and operationalization of a framework for learning and data in smart cities and regions. As illustrated in Fig. 5.2, through the interactive dynamic of *people—technologies—cities,* learning is explored through the proxy of community participation in relation to learning infrastructures and knowledge and data infrastructures in smart cities contributing to emergent understandings of learning cities, involving factors pertaining to privacy, security, and trust.

This exploration of learning and data in smart cities gives rise to the research question, in twenty-first century cities:

Q1: How does *learning* pertain to data in smarter city initiatives?

The research question is reformulated here as a proposition for exploration in this chapter, as follows.

P1: *Learning* pertains to data in smarter city initiatives on many levels, across many sectors including learning infrastructures and knowledge infrastructures associated with people and data privacy, security, and trust.

5.4 Methodology

The research design for this chapter included an exploratory case study approach incorporating multiple methods of data collection including an online survey and in-depth interviews combined with an explanatory correlations design. The process, data sources, and analysis techniques for the study underlying this chapter are described in Sects. 5.4.1–5.4.3.

5.4.1   Process

A website was used to describe the study, enable sign up, the gathering of basic demographic data, and self-identification in one or more categories (e.g., educator, student, community member, city official, business, and other). Participants were invited to complete an online survey and engage in an in-depth interview enabling discussion of their experience of learning in their city or community. This study attracted interest from individuals across several continents in multiple countries including Canada, United States, Israel, and Ireland, to name a few.

5.4.2   Sources of Evidence

A survey instrument and interview protocol were developed and pre-tested prior to use in the study with questions focusing on learning, data, and factors associated with privacy, security, and trust.

In parallel with this study, evidence was systematically gathered from diverse voices (e.g., city officials, business, educators, students, community members, and IT staff) across Canadian cities (e.g., Toronto, Vancouver, Victoria) enabling further triangulation and enriching of data.

5.4.3   Data Analysis

Content analysis was employed using a combination of deductive analysis based on terminology from the research literature and inductive analysis of qualitative data collected from in-depth interviews, open ended survey questions, and group and individual discussions in the identification of patterns. Descriptive statistics were used to analyze data gathered from survey questions while functionality in the Real Statistics software package add in for Microsoft Excel [26] enabled the conducting of correlations between *learning*, using *community participation* as a proxy, and factors pertaining to data such as *privacy*, *security*, and *trust*.

Overall, an analysis was conducted for $n = 78$ consisting of 41% females and 59% males for people ranging in age from their 20s to 70s.

5.5   Findings

Findings are presented in response to the research question based on the proposition investigated in terms of *learning* using the proxy of *community participation*. Table 5.2 shows learning responses using a seven-point Likert-type scale with

Table 5.2 Community participation responses assessed for the making of smart cities

Variables	1	2	3	4	5	6	7
Community participation						25%	75%

Table 5.3 Privacy, security, and trust responses assessed in relation to data in smart cities

Variables	1	2	3	4	5	6	7
Privacy						50%	50%
Security						50%	50%
Trust						25%	75%

1 = not at all and 7 = absolutely, pertaining to *community participation* as a proxy for *learning* in the city, with 25% toward the upper end of the scale at position 6 and 75% at the upper position of 7.

Privacy, security, and trust are assessed in relation to data in smart cities and Table 5.3 shows responses for privacy with 50% at position 6 and 50% at position 7; for security with 50% at position 6 and 50% at position 7; and for trust with 25% at position 6 and 75% at position 7.

The Spearman Correlation Coefficient for ordinal data is then conducted for privacy, security, and trust in relation to learning using *community participation* as a proxy with Table 5.4 showing the results when correlated with *privacy* as inverse at −.57.

Table 5.5 shows assessments for *learning* using *community participation* as a proxy when correlated with *security,* resulting in a negative, inverse correlation of −57.

Table 5.6 shows assessments for *learning* using *community participation* as a proxy that, when correlated with *trust,* result in a negative, inverse correlation of −.33.

Exploring further, Table 5.7 shows assessments for *learning* using *community participation* as a proxy when correlated with *visual ways to show success in real time,* resulting in a negative, inverse correlation of −.33.

It is worth noting that when asked what cities need to do to become smarter, 83% chose the option to "support learning cities by enabling new forms and configurations for education in the city (e.g., school-university-city collaborations, etc.)"

In terms of what people said, qualitatively, comments on learning in smart cities emerged in a variety of ways. For example, regarding what contributes to the making of a smart city, a student stated, "participation more than anything." A public administrator highlighted the importance of "learning capabilities" and the "need for a learning strategy" along with "learning via interconnections with other cities" contributing to the making of smart cities. An educator suggested that "learning can be integrated into smart cities by thinking of cities as learning ecologies" in support of "discovery, sociability and connectedness." An educator and business person expressed preference for the term "wise city" where collaboration is enabled through "place-based projects" and students could participate in smart city initiatives and "make a real contribution" if "schools open their 'walls'." Another educator

Table 5.4 Correlating assessments for *community participation* and *privacy* in smart cities

Items	Assessments	Correlation
Community participation	25% (6); 75% (7)	−.57
Privacy	50% (5); 50% (7)	

Table 5.5 Assessments for community participation and security

Items	Assessments	Correlation
Community participation	25% (6); 75% (7)	−.57
Security	50% (5); 50% (7)	

Table 5.6 Assessments for community participation and trust

Items	Assessments	Correlation
Community participation	25% (6); 75% (7)	−.33
Trust	25% (5); 75% (7)	

Table 5.7 Assessments for community participation & visual ways to show success

Items	Assessments	Correlation
Community participation	25% (6); 75% (7)	−.33
Visual ways to show success in real time	25% (6); 75% (7)	

highlighted the importance of "collaboration projects between public authorities and community groups where citizens are considered partners" adding that "adoption of technologies, community weaving, trust relationships between the authorities and the public make all the difference."

A community member in Greater Victoria stated that "when I'm walking around the park or in different places, little boards that explain something about the birds around there or nature are the most tangible example of a learning city that I see in the physical environment" and "just talking to people or discovering" what is going on "around the city." City IT staff highlighted the phenomena of "accidental data collection" and data that "I don't think anybody saw a need for." Additionally, it was noted that "we're starting to look at the tools to help us mine the data that we already have an interest in" and "beyond that, we're very much immature in that overall data sense." Further, City IT pointed to data "between two different datasets" and how "we're just starting to look at the tools that would give us the visualization of that" while highlighting "that hurdle of just really starting to educate" about "what could be done" and "educating ourselves" adding that, "we haven't had any kind of funding to do these things."

Learning was envisioned by a community member based on the use of technologies "to experience the city in a different way" in terms of "the environment or the history" to "create different games or opportunities for people" and to "make cities more friendly for our kids." This individual commented that "there is a whole other layer that could be added in order to make the city more usable for everybody." A student and educator referred to "geofenced location based content" that is "connected in relation to community interactions" while noting that "learning becomes a subsumed subtext of what you are doing everyday, all the time" as in "you are all learning all the time" and "you're sharing knowledge" adding that "it might be formal, informal, it might be fun, it might be serious." University-community initiatives were highlighted with "events on the environment or healthy eating" as an example of learning in London "in terms of being smart in a liveable way." A community member in St. John's observed that "we're not smart on how we use the technology" suggesting that "improved communications about the transportation system" and "anywhere Internet" are key priorities that would be "particularly useful."

5.6 Discussion: Enhancing Data Literacies in Smart Cities

A discussion of findings is presented in relation to the proposition explored quantitatively and qualitatively in this chapter. It is worth recalling that according to Creswell [27], for correlations in the "range from .20 to .35, there is only a slight relationship" while those in the .35–.65 range "are useful for limited prediction" while Yin [28] reminds us that "case studies have been needed to examine the underlying processes that might explain a correlation."

Figure 5.3 shows the correlations found between *learning* using *community participation* as a proxy and other factors in smart cities such as *privacy, security,* and *trust* as well as *visual ways to show success in real time.* While correlations between *learning* using *community participation* as a proxy and factors such as data *privacy,* $(-.57)$ *security* $(-.57)$ and *trust* $(-.33)$, emerge as negative or inverse, qualitative data may assist in shedding light on these findings.

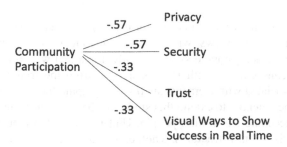

Fig. 5.3 Correlations for learning as community participation in relation to data

For example, regarding trust, in a number of instances, participants cited the need for meaningful citizen participation as "partners" and the importance of "trust relationships" suggestive perhaps of the ongoing need voiced by Weber [22] for cities to be more "inhabitant-centric." As such, findings in this chapter would seem to be suggesting that as community participation occurs, people are learning more about the challenges and opportunities of smart cities and this may explain in part concerns with privacy, security, and trust as learning increases. This inverse relationship gives rise to the need, as suggested by one participant, for "learning capabilities" as part of "a learning strategy" and the incorporation of "community weaving" into smart city initiatives as suggested by another.

Similarly, when probing further to explore *community participation* as *learning* when correlated with *visual ways to show success in real time,* an inverse relationship of $-.33$ again emerges. Qualitatively, it is worth noting the advice by an educator who called for "data visualisations in real time" with smart referring to "social, useful, and having clear purpose" as distinct from data displays that are described by another educator as "merely advertising" reminiscent perhaps of the notion of "impression management" [23].

As such, this overview is intended to contribute to urban infrastructural improvements for learning involving elements such as: community participants as partners; learning from other cities (e.g., networks) as advanced by Castro [19], and accounting for knowledge and resources as advanced by Manchester and Cope [16]. As city administration, business, community members, educators, students, and people in the city generally become more collaborative, the potential emerges for increased learning by everyone involved, in relation to the development of "strategies" for interacting with each other and with aware technologies in more meaningful ways, creating greater success potentials for smart cities generally and for the notion of learning cities in particular.

5.7 Limitations, Mitigations, and Implications

A key limitation of the work in this chapter is the small sample size and this is mitigated by in-depth interviews with diverse individuals across multiple cities. Additionally, evidence gathered systematically in parallel with this study, contributes further richness along with increased rigor from the triangulation of data. Limitations associated with elements such as geographic location and city size are mitigated by the potential to extend this study to other cities and mega-regions with populations exceeding ten million people. Understanding the nature of embedded and often less visible infrastructures, whether digital (e.g., in the form of algorithms, social media, and the like) or human (e.g., in the form of learning and social interactions), presented challenges that are mitigated by in-depth discussion and real world examples. Using community participation as a proxy for learning may also contribute to limitations in this chapter.

5.7.1 Implications for Practice and Research

Going forward this chapter has implications for practice and research in terms of learning and data in the context of smart cities and learning cities discussed below.

Learning and Data: Implications for Practice

This chapter highlights learning challenges for practitioners in smart cities by presenting three key opportunities, as follows:

1. *Learning infrastructures.* Expanding understandings of learning infrastructures to include human infrastructures in relation to digital and data infrastructures that are aware, interactive, and adaptive.
2. *Participation and Collaboration as Learning.* Initiatives for smart cities and regions that meaningfully involve community participants, contributing to learning for everyone involved in the context of more aware people interacting with each other and with aware technologies.
3. *Learning and data.* Providing increased learning opportunities for the creative and meaningful generation, processing, and use of new data streams enabled by sensing, sensors, the IoT, social media, and other aware technologies, contributing to increased knowledge, resources, value, and success in smart cities and regions.

Learning and Data: Implications for Research

This chapter contributes to the evolving of urban theory and approaches to methodology for researchers by identifying three directions for future research, as follows:

1. *Learning and aware technology environments.* Explore the leveraging of human learning capabilities through more meaningful community participation to complement and extend the technical capabilities of aware technologies in urban spaces.
2. *Lifelong and lifewide learning.* Further exploration of learning as lifelong and lifewide encompassing all aspects of smart cities and regions in support of learning and knowledge infrastructures accommodating learning cities.
3. *Real world, real time data and learning.* Further development, exploration, and theorizing of the learning concept focusing on real world, real time interactions, initiatives, and issues—including but not limited to privacy, security, and trust.

In summary, challenges and opportunities for explorations of learning and data in smart cities are presented in Table 5.8 in terms of practice and research.

Findings in terms of challenges for practice include partnering for learning in smart cities; partnering in the visualizing of urban data; and collaborating for learning as seeing through smart cities.

Table 5.8 Challenges & opportunities for explorations of learning & data in smart cities

	Practice	Research
Challenges	Partnering for learning in smart cities	Learning and urban data
	Partnering in visualizing urban data	Learning and smart cities
	Collaborating for learning as seeing	Meaningful participation in smart city initiatives
Opportunities	Leveraging learning in the city by people	Learning about potential uses for public data
	Strategies for learning involving people	Learning & knowledge infrastructures in SCs
	Learning as appropriating smart cities	Learning ecologies for: people, data & technologies

Insights	The nature of the relationship between learning and data factors in smart cities as inverse
Patterns	Negative, inverse relationships between learning and data related factors (e.g., privacy, etc.)
Spaces for dialogue	Meaningful community participation as learning, influencing smart city initiatives
Urban theory/ methods	Approaches featuring learning in technology-aware environments

For research, challenges include learning in relation to urban data; understanding learning in smart cities; and understandings of meaningful participation in smart city initiatives. For practice, opportunities include leveraging learning in the city through people; leveraging strategies for learning involving people; and learning as appropriating understandings of smart cities. For research, opportunities include learning about potential uses for public data; learning and knowledge infrastructures in smart cities; and learning ecologies for people, data, and technologies.

Table 5.8 also includes key insights, patterns, spaces for dialogue, and urban theory and methods. A key insight from this chapter is the nature of the relationships between learning and data factors in smart cities as negative or inverse, in relation privacy, security, and trust. As such, among the patterns emerging in this chapter is the absence of any positive correlations between learning and data associated factors and the persistence of negative, inverse relationships in the learning space in relation to data. Given such patterns, spaces for dialogue emerge in this chapter for meaningful community participation as learning, influencing smart city initiatives, extending possibly to approaches involving learning for urban theory and methods in technology-aware environments. As such, Table 5.8 serves to further support elements highlighted from the literature review in Fig. 5.1 in terms of learning infrastructures, lifewide learning, and interactive data and urban learning in smart cities, to name a few.

5.8 Conclusion

This chapter uses a literature review followed by a combined exploratory case study approach combined with an explanatory correlational design to conduct an investigation of learning in relation to data related factors such as privacy, security, and trust in the context of smart cities and learning cities. The significance of this chapter is associated with explorations of learning and data as a way of seeing and understanding smart cities. This chapter contributes to: the research literature for learning cities; urban theory in further developing and extending understandings of the importance of learning infrastructures and knowledge infrastructures in smart cities; and approaches to the study of learning cities and data involving assessments by people based on their experiences of smart cities and regions. This work has implications going forward for: (a) practice, making recommendations related to: learning infrastructures; participation and collaboration as learning; and learning and data and (b) research, making recommendations related to: learning and aware technology environments; lifelong and lifewide learning; and real world, real time data and learning. A key take-away from this work is the negative or inverse relationship found between learning and data related factors in smart cities. This finding opens opportunities for research and practice to improve learning infrastructures and knowledge infrastructures to complement the development and maintenance of existing and emergent physical, service, and digital urban infrastructures in support of success for smart cities. Indeed, learning as community participation, informing knowledge infrastructures has the potential to influence practice and research agendas in smart cities and regions. This chapter will be of interest to a broad audience including community members, academics, students, city officials, business, community leaders, urban professionals and anyone concerned with learning and data in support of learning cities and smart cities and regions. As such, three questions are raised for educators, students, and community leaders, as follows:

Q 5.1. What would you say is missing from this exploration of learning as a way of seeing through smart cities? And what would your key question or questions be?
Q 5.2. How would you describe learning in a smart city or region?
Q 5.3. Is learning and data important for smart cities and regions? Please explain briefly why or why not.

If you would like to share your responses to these questions with the author of this book an online space is provided here [https://forms.gle/Y6FFkzahTX5NL T4A7].

References

1. Nam, T., & Pardo, T. A. (2011). Conceptualizing smart city with dimensions of technology, people, and institutions. In *Proceedings of the 12th Annual Conference on Digital Government*.
2. Ferronato, P., & Ruecker, S. (2018). Smart citizenship: Designing the interaction between citizens and smart cities. In C. Storni, K. Leahy, M. McMahon, P. Lloyd, & E. Bohemia (Eds.),

Design as a catalyst for change—DRS International Conference 2018, 25–28 June, Limerick, Ireland. https://doi.org/10.21606/drs.2018.480

3. Ismagilova, E., Hughes, L., Rana, N. P., & Dwivedi, Y. K. (2020). Security, privacy and risks within smart cities: Literature review and development of a smart city interaction framework. *Information Systems Frontiers.* https://doi.org/10.1007/s10796-020-10044-1

4. Tavmen, G. (2020, July). Data/infrastructure in the smart city: Understanding the infrastructural power of Citymapper app through technicity of data. *Big Data & Society, 7*(2), 1–15. https://doi.org/10.1177/2053951720965618

5. Merriam-Webster. (2020). *Dictionary, thesaurus.* Retrieved November 14, 2020, from https://www.merriam-webster.com/dictionary/data

6. Merriam-Webster. (2020). *Dictionary, thesaurus.* Retrieved November 14, 2020, from https://www.merriam-webster.com/dictionary/privacy

7. Merriam-Webster. (2020). *Dictionary, thesaurus.* Retrieved November 14, 2020, from https://www.merriam-webster.com/dictionary/security

8. Merriam-Webster. (2020). *Dictionary, thesaurus.* Retrieved November 14, 2020, from https://www.merriam-webster.com/dictionary/trust

9. UNESCO. (2017). *UNESCO global network of learning cities.* Retrieved August 23, 2020, from https://uil.unesco.org/lifelong-learning/learning-cities

10. Borgman, C. L., Edwards, P. N., Jackson, S. J., Chalmers, M. K., Bowker, G. C., Ribes, D., … Calvert, S. (2013). *Knowledge infrastructures: Intellectual frameworks and research challenges.* Report of a workshop sponsored by the National Science Foundation and the Sloan Foundation, University of Michigan School of Information, 25–28 May 2012.

11. Borgman, C. L., Darch, P. T., Pasquetto, I. V., & Wofford, M. F. (2020). *Our knowledge of knowledge infrastructures: Lessons learned and future directions.* Report of Knowledge Infrastructures Workshop, 5 June 2020, UCLA. Funded by the Alfred P. Sloan Foundation, Data and Computational Research Program.

12. Zhuang, R., Fang, H., Zhang, Y., Lu, A., & Huang, R. (2017). Smart learning environments for a smart city: From the perspective of lifelong and lifewide learning. *Smart Learning Environments, 4*(5), 6. https://doi.org/10.1186/s40561-017-0044-8

13. Facer, K., & Buchczyk, M. (2019). Towards a research agenda for the 'actually existing' learning city. Editorial. *Oxford Review of Education, 45*(2), 151–167, Special Issue on Learning Cities. https://doi.org/10.1080/03054985.2018.1551990

14. Facer, K., & Buchczyk, M. (2019). Understanding learning cities as discursive, material and affective infrastructures. *Oxford Review of Education, 45*(2), 168–187. Special Issue on Learning Cities. https://doi.org/10.1080/03054985.2018.1552581

15. Lido, C., Reid, K., & Osborne, M. (2019). Lifewide learning in the city: Novel big data approaches to exploring learning with large-scale surveys, GPS, and social media. *Oxford Review of Education, 45*(2), 279–295. Special Issue on Learning Cities. https://doi.org/10.1080/03054985.218.1554531

16. Manchester, H., & Cope, G. (2019). Learning to be a smart citizen. *Oxford Review of Education, 45*(2), 224–241. Special Issue on Learning Cities. https://doi.org/10.1080/03054985.2018.1552582

17. Lister, P. (2020). Smart learning in the community: Supporting citizen digital skills and literacies. In N. Streitz & S. Konomi (Eds.), *Distributed, ambient and pervasive interactions. HCII 2020. Lecture notes in computer science* (Vol. 12203). Cham: Springer. https://doi.org/10.1007/978-3-030-50344-4_38

18. Chauncey, S. A., & Simpson, G. I. (2020). The role of learning city "smart teams" in promoting, supporting, and extending the community school model. In C. Stephanidis et al. (Eds.), *HCI International 2020—Late breaking papers: Cognition, learning and games. HCII 2020. Lecture notes in computer science* (Vol. 12425). Cham: Springer. https://doi.org/10.1007/978-3-030-60128-7_25

19. Castro, D. (2017, September). *Building the learning city: Networks of smart cities will help make the most of data-driven governing.* GovTech. Retrieved August 22, 2020, from https://www.govtech.com/data/GT-September-2017-Building-the-Learning-City.html

20. McKenna, H. P. (2017). Civic tech and ambient data in the public realm. In N. Streitz & P. Markopoulos (Eds.), *Distributed, ambient and pervasive interactions. DAPI 2017. Lecture notes in computer science* (Vol. 10291). Cham: Springer. https://doi.org/10.1007/978-3-319-58697-7_2

21. McKenna, H. P. (2019). Getting smarter about data and access in smart cities. In M. Antona & C. Stephanidis (Eds.), *Universal access in human-computer interaction. Theory, methods and tools. HCII 2019. Lecture notes in computer science* (Vol. 11572). Cham: Springer. https://doi.org/10.1007/978-3-030-23560-4_11

22. Weber, V. (2019, April 16). *Smart cities must pay more attention to the people who live in them.* World Economic Forum Agenda. Retrieved August 22, 2020, from https://www.weforum.org/agenda/2019/04/why-smart-cities-should-listen-to-residents/

23. Currie, M. (2020). Data as performance—Showcasing cities through open data maps. *Big Data & Society, 7*(1), 1–14. https://doi.org/10.1177/2053951720907953

24. Sophus Lai, S., & Flensburg, S. (2020, July). A proxy for privacy uncovering the surveillance ecology of mobile apps. *Big Data & Society*. https://doi.org/10.1177/2053951720942543

25. Bowe, E., Simmons, E., & Mattern, S. (2020, July). Learning from lines: Critical COVID data visualizations and the quarantine quotidian. *Big Data & Society*. https://doi.org/10.1177/2053951720939236

26. Zaiontz, C. (2020). *Real statistics using excel.* Retrieved from www.real-statistics.com

27. Creswell, J. W. (2018). *Educational research: Planning, conducting, and evaluating quantitative and qualitative research* (6th ed.). Boston, MA: Pearson.

28. Yin, R. K. (2018). *Case study research and applications: Design and methods.* Thousand Oaks, CA: Sage.

Chapter 6
Openness and Data Access in Smart Cities

6.1 Introduction

The focus of this chapter is on openness and data in real time, in the context of smart cities. Gil-Garcia, Puron-Cid, and Zhang [1] identify openness as one of 14 dimensions of smartness in government. Hawken, Han, and Pettit, [2] claim that while cities are "the platform for the infotech giants" it would seem that cities "have been slow to catch onto the idea that it is their data rather than any new tech infrastructure, that is the most valuable asset." And so it is, that Hawken et al. [2] speak of "a critical moment for open cities" in terms of "the information economy as a powerful transformational force" with cities being "active in positioning, advocating and shaping the Open Data economy." In terms of challenges and opportunities, Hawken et al. [2] remind us that "what data to open up and how to open up that data are not straightforward questions." As such, this chapter explores the research literature for openness and data access in smart cities. Using an exploratory case study approach combined with an explanatory correlational design, the smart city experiences of people are investigated as well as their assessments for openness, data access, privacy, trust, and connecting.

6.2 Background

Nam and Pardo [3] identify "levels of interaction" in smart cities initiatives where "objects of interaction" are said to include "data, information, and knowledge." Pomerantz and Peek [4] review the term "open" in many contexts from open access to open society to open government, in describing how open means a range of things from access, to use, to participatory while enabling openness. Lehtinen and Vihanninjoki [5] claim that "the urban everyday is not only the realm of logical and

© Springer Nature Switzerland AG 2021
H. P. McKenna, *Seeing Smart Cities Through a Multi-Dimensional Lens*
https://doi.org/10.1007/978-3-030-70821-4_6

rational efficiency but also open to the human qualities such as emotions, imagination, and different types of unanticipated quirks" and as such, this chapter argues that all realms contribute to urban data. The objective of this chapter then is to explores openness, data, and data access in the context of smart cities, giving rise to the research question:

Q1: Why does *openness* matter for data access in smart cities?

Providing additional context for this work, key terms are defined in Sect. 6.2.1.

6.2.1   Definitions

Definitions for key terms used in this chapter are provided beginning with openness, based on the research literature for smart cities. Definitions for other associated terms are provided, such as access, big data, open data, and privacy.

Openness

Gil-Garcia et al. [1] describe openness as "a key dimension characterizing smartness in government" adding that "when a government is open, it becomes more transparent and more accountable" and as such, "a smarter government for its citizens, businesses, and other stakeholders" while using "diverse information in smarter ways."

Access

Merriam-Webster Dictionary defines access as "freedom or ability to obtain or make use of something" [6].

Big Data

Hawken et al. [2] refer to big data as "what businesses and governments use to know how you think and trace what you do."

Open Data

Hawken et al. [2] describe open data as "a conscious act that releases and presents data in a way that anyone can use" and as such "is an investment in society" and "is often the intelligent use of Big Data for public purposes."

Privacy

Merriam-Webster Dictionary defines privacy as "freedom from unauthorized intrusion" [7].

6.3   Openness and Data in Smart Cities: A Theoretical Perspective

The openness concept as a dimension of seeing smart cities is explored and developed in this chapter through a review of the research literature in relation to open data; to data and access; to policy, governance, and regulation; and to privacy and sharing. This review of the research literature will also be attentive to challenges and opportunities for openness and data access in smart cities.

6.3.1   Open Data and Smart Cities

Hawken et al. [2] refer to "Dimensions of Open Data" including elements such as, "accessibility, interactivity, legibility, accuracy, and timeliness" that are said to be key to forming "healthy information ecosystems." Harkins and Heard [8] note that while "data sets can be either open or proprietary" where "the generally accepted definition of Open Data refers to publicly available data" their work offers a "slightly different interpretation" by referring to "how proprietary data sets can be shared among commercial entities freely, for efficiency and mutually beneficial outcomes." For example, "building data" in the form of "privately owned data sets" are needed to "better inform how our smart cities operate by considering the individuals daily activities" which "is driving private companies to open their data and make it accessible for public use" [8]. Trindade Neves, de Castro Neto, and Aparicio [9] explore the impact of open data initiatives on smart cities, providing a theoretical framework for impact evaluation taking city context into consideration. It is worth noting that Trindade Neves et al. [9] draw attention to a set of open data impact elements by Verhulst and Young [10], one of which is "open washing", described as "awareness of the mismatch between public expectations and government transparency on data publication." Regarding open data, de Waal, de Lange, and Bouw [11] argue that "data need to be offered in ways that make it understandable and actionable."

6.3.2   Data and Access in Smart Cities

Mattern [12] provides a glimpse of the contested nature of data access, governance, and civic engagement in a smart city project in progress by Sidewalk Labs in the city of Toronto, which has since been cancelled, due it is said to the global COVID-19 pandemic. Pointing to "the increasing amount of data being generated by our cities" Harkins and Heard [8] describe the "underlying layer of data and information" and argue for "creating interfaces that can access and represent this data in a more human readable form." For Harkins and Heard [8] the interface is critical since, without it, "there is no way to interact with the invisible 0s and 1s that make up the data being held within our devices." Additionally, according to Harkins and Heard [8], "as more and more people are becoming aware of this underlying data" what is emerging "is a growing desire to access and use this information to our benefit as a population." Because "there is no universal way to easily interact with this information" rendering it seemingly "inaccessible, confusing, masked, or hidden" such that "where there are ways to gain access, the data is rarely, if ever, contextualized in a meaningful way for non-skilled users to understand", Harkins and Heard [8] propose "creating accessible virtual environments" for "buildings and cities, using design processes such as BIM" as in, Building Information Modelling. In this way "game engine technology" is said to provide "a unique method of interfacing with huge data sets" with "gamification" providing "the basis for these virtual worlds" that are "enhanced with rich metadata" thus "providing a visual platform for everyday users to better understand the context and availability of the data woven inextricably into the fabric of our cities" [8].

6.3.3   Policy, Governance, and Regulation in Smart Cities

In the context of smart cities, Lea [13] describes open data as "public policy that requires or encourages public agencies to release data sets and make them freely accessible." However, while Lea [14] refers to open data as "powerful" it is also described as "often 'low value' data" because it is "mostly infrastructure centric or anonymized in such a way to ensure privacy, but reduce usefulness" and Lea [14] proposes the notion of a "data brokerage" as a solution for both organizational data and citizen data. Hawken et al. [2] point to the importance of policy, governance, and regulation associated with open data in smart cities while Van Zoonen [15] highlights the challenges associated with "data-driven" or "data steering" for data governance, drawing on the "discourse of steering" literature by Engelbert [16], if citizen participation is to be accommodated. It is perhaps worth noting that the Smart Data and Smart Cities Conference 2020 defines a smart city as "a city overlaid by a digital skin which is used not only for storing city information but overall for its governance" adding that "a smart city cannot be defined without a better involvement and connection of its citizens (smart people)" [17].

6.3.4 Privacy and Sharing in Smart Cities

From a legal perspective, Solove [18] argues that "privacy is a construct in disarray" and provides a taxonomy "to understand privacy problems." Van Zoonen [19] employs a privacy framework using the two dimensions of data type as personal or impersonal and the purpose of data as surveillance or service, based on recurring concerns expressed by people in smart cities. Curzon, Almehmadi, and El-Khatib [20] provide a review of privacy enhancing technologies for smart cities. Privacy is, according to the Institute for Foundations of Data Science (IFDS) (2020) [21], "a continuing challenge in data science" and Stephens [21] indicates that the Institute seeks "to investigate ways to protect the privacy of individuals while allowing access to large genomic data sets." Solove (2021) [22] challenges the "privacy paradox" claiming it to be "a myth created by faulty logic." According to Solove [22], "managing one's privacy is a vast, complex, and never-ending project that does not scale" so that instead of "privacy regulation to give people more privacy self-management", Solove recommends "regulating the architecture that structures the way information is used, maintained, and transferred."

6.3.5 Summary

In summary, this review of the literature highlights the importance of openness for smart cities, along with issues associated with data and data access. As outlined in Table 6.1, Solove [18] seeks to provide an understanding of privacy problems through a taxonomy for privacy.

Nam and Pardo [3] identify data and information as objects of interaction in smart cities while Gil-Garcia et al. [1] identify openness as a key dimension of

Table 6.1 Overview of openness and data in smart cities as challenges and opportunities

Author(s)	Year	Challenges	Opportunities
Solove	2006	Taxonomy for understanding privacy problems	
Nam & Pardo	2011	Objects of interaction—data, information, etc.	
Gil-Garcia et al.	2016	Openness and smartness in government	
Lea	2018	Open data as public policy	
Curzon et al.	2019	Privacy enhancing technologies	
Lea	2019	Data brokerage for open data	
de Waal et al.	2020	Open data—understandable & actionable	
Harkins & Heard	2020	Interface & the data layer	Data access & use; VR
Hawken et al.	2020	Open data and what data to open and how	
Mattern	2020	Data governance and civic participation	
Trindade et al.	2020	Open data initiatives—impact	
Van Zoonen	2020	Data-driven/data steering discourse & citizen participation	
Solove	2021	Managing privacy	

Practice / Research		
Challenges	Defining urban openness	
	Openness infrastructures	
	People, privacy, and data interactions	
Opportunities	Data Access	
	Openness infrastructures	
	Data privacy architectures	

Fig. 6.1 Challenges and opportunities for openness and data in smart cities

smartness in government. Lea [13] discusses open data as public policy while Curzon et al. [20] provide an overview of privacy enhancing technologies. Lea [14] advances the notion of a data brokerage for open data as a way to mitigate issues associated with privacy and value. de Waal et al. [11] stress that open data from cities must be "understandable and actionable" for "citymaking" initiatives. Harkins and Heard [8] point to the importance of open data for access and use, acknowledging challenges of what data to open up and how. Mattern [12] highlights the contested nature of data in smart cities and meaningfully involving people in civic design. Trindade et al. [9] explore the impact of open data initiatives for smart cities through monitoring and evaluation. Van Zoonen [15] focuses on challenges associated with the discourse of data-driven or data-steering if citizen participation is to be accommodated. Solove [22] takes issue with the privacy paradox notion proposing instead a different approach to the challenge of privacy management as an opportunity for the regulators of information architectures.

Viewed another way, as depicted in Fig. 6.1, challenges emerge for both practice and research in relation to openness in everyday spaces that may also be technology embedded environments, giving rise to challenges and opportunities associated with data. Challenges include defining urban openness; openness infrastructures; and people, privacy, and data interactions. Opportunities include data access; openness infrastructures; and data privacy architectures.

6.3.6 Conceptual Framework for Openness and Data in Smart Cities

The theoretical perspective developed in this chapter provides a background and context for development, theorizing, and operationalization of a conceptual framework for openness and data in smart cities and regions. As illustrated in Fig. 6.2, through the interactive dynamic of *people—technologies—cities,* openness is explored in relation to urban data through access, privacy, trust, connecting, and

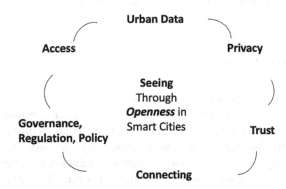

Fig. 6.2 Conceptual framework for openness and data in smart cities

governance, regulation, and policy in smart cities, contributing to emergent understandings of seeing.

The research question identified in Sect. 6.2 is reformulated here as a proposition for exploration in this chapter, as follows.

P1: *Openness* matters for data access in smart cities as data becomes more critical, complex, and valuable requiring ever more creativity associated with policy, governance, regulation, privacy, and connecting.

6.4   Methodology

The research design for this chapter included an exploratory case study approach incorporating multiple methods of data collection including survey and in-depth interviews in combination with an explanatory correlational design. In support of this approach, the process, data sources, and analysis techniques for this study are described in Sects. 6.4.1–6.4.3.

6.4.1   Process

A website was used to describe the study, enable sign up, the gathering of basic demographic data, including self-identification in one or more categories (e.g., educator, student, community member, city official, business, and other). Participants were invited to complete an online survey and engage in an in-depth discussion of their experience of openness in their city or community. This study attracted interest from individuals in cities in Canada, extending to cities in other countries such as the United States, Israel, and Ireland, to name a few.

6.4.2   Sources of Evidence

An interview protocol and a survey instrument were developed and pre-tested prior to use in the study underlying this chapter, that included questions pertaining to openness and data and associated factors in smart cities and regions.

In parallel with this study, data were systematically gathered from diverse voices (e.g., city officials, business, educators, students, community members, and IT staff) in a number of Canadian cities (e.g., Toronto, Vancouver, Victoria) enabling further triangulation and enriching of data.

6.4.3   Data Analysis

Content analysis was employed using a combination of deductive analysis based on terminology from the research literature and inductive analysis of qualitative data collected from study participants in open-ended survey questions and in-depth interviews. Descriptive statistics were used to analyze assessments of openness data and associated factors gathered from survey questions while the Real Statistics add-in for Microsoft Excel [23] was used to conduct correlations between items to determine the Spearman correlation coefficient for ordinal data.

Overall, an analysis was conducted for n = 78 consisting of 41% females and 59% males for people ranging in age from their 20s to 70s.

6.5   Findings

Findings are presented in response to the research question based on an exploration of the proposition in terms of assessments for *openness* and *access to public data, privacy, trust,* and *connecting.* As shown in Table 6.2, assessments of *openness* as contributing to the making of smart cities, using a seven-point Likert-type scale with 1 = not at all and 7 = absolutely, yields 25% of responses occurring toward the upper end of the scale at position 5 and 75% at the upper position of 7.

Table 6.2 Openness responses assessed for contributing to the making of smart cities

Variables	1	2	3	4	5	6	7
Openness					25%		75%

Table 6.3 Access to public data assessed as a factor contributing to livability in smart cities

Variables	1	2	3	4	5	6	7
Access to public data				25%	25%	25%	25%

Table 6.4 Correlating assessments for openness and access to public data (livability)

Items	Assessments	Correlation
Openness	25% (5); 75% (7)	.77
Access to public data	25% (4); 25% (5); 25% (6); 25% (7)	

Assessments are then explored for *access to public data* as a factor contributing to the livability of a smart city as shown in Table 6.3. Responses for assessments of *access to public data* occur evenly at 25% across positions 4–7 on the scale.

Using the Real Statistics Software add-in for Microsoft Excel [23], a correlation is conducted between *openness* as an element contributing to the making of smart cities and *access to public data* as a factor contributing to livability, showing a positive Spearman correlation coefficient for ordinal data in Table 6.4, of .77.

Exploring further to investigate *openness* in relation to *privacy*, Table 6.5 shows assessment responses for *privacy* (as contributing to increased value for data) of 50% at position 6 and 50% at position 7. When correlated with *openness*, *privacy* shows a positive Spearman correlation coefficient of .57.

Exploring further to investigate *openness* in relation to *trust*, Table 6.6 shows assessment responses for *trust* (in relation to potentials for city-focused social media and other aware technologies) of 25% at position 5, 25% at position 6 and 50% at position 7. When correlated with *openness*, *trust* shows a positive Spearman correlation coefficient of .36.

Exploring further to investigate *openness* in relation to *connecting*, Table 6.7 shows assessment responses for *connecting* (in relation to potentials for city-focused social media and other aware technologies) of 17% at position 5 and 83% at position 7. When correlated with *openness*, *connecting* shows a positive Spearman correlation coefficient of .63.

To shed further light on quantitative findings, what people said in open-ended survey questions, interviews, and group and individual discussions, is provided below.

When asked, "what do you like about being in the city?" an educator and business person responded with, "the sense of freedom and openness." An educator referred to social media and other emergent technology data streams as a kind of "back channel" or "transmission zone." City IT staff commented that "fundamentally there is a desire to be very, very open with the available data" as public data. It was noted that, "the other element we're trying to share is even just the processes of City Hall" such as permit applications. City IT staff added that open, diverse datasets enable "data analysis that you've not thought of" enabling the potential for "serendipitous or accidental usage" or "unintended usage" and unforeseen value. Providing an example from business, usage revealed, "a win that wasn't even in our mindset" where staff "were using" real-time information "as a predictive piece to

Table 6.5 Correlation for assessments of openness and privacy

Items	Assessments	Correlation
Openness	25% (5); 75% (7)	.57
Privacy	50% (6); 50% (7)	

Table 6.6 Correlation for assessments of openness and trust

Items	Assessments	Correlation
Openness	25% (5); 75% (7)	.36
Trust	25% (5); 25% (6); 50% (7)	

Table 6.7 Correlation for assessments of openness and connecting

Items	Assessments	Correlation
Openness	25% (5); 75% (7)	.63
Connecting	17% (5); 83% (7)	

inform their daily operations." In response to what contributes to the making of a smart city, a public administrator highlighted the importance of "having a say on the governance" adding that more could be done "in terms of governance" with social media and other aware technologies. An educator suggested "the usefulness of what might be provided through technology and access to information." An educator and business person pointed to the need for schools to "open their 'walls'" in getting people more involved in the city and the community. A community leader pointed to the importance of "finding fun and meaningful ways to engage the public and visualize this data, and 'simplify' it for the larger public" and "make it about more than data." An educator speaks of the smart city "as a playful and open territory of personal and community development."

Referring to public Internet access, a community member observed that "not everybody is going to have a data plan, its expensive and to be able to have that at your fingertips and have it be just part of a city service is actually incredible." City IT commented that, "we are interested in putting physical infrastructure in place" and "how we interpret using it is still open," identifying challenges that include jurisdictional ones in terms of "a hard stop at municipal boundaries." In terms of wicked challenges, a student identified "control" issues such as "who owns the data, how is it housed, and the infrastructure by which it is shared" pointing the way perhaps to the architecture regulation recommendation by Solove [22]. The student highlighted the potential for data to be "open and shared in some way that would still provide some kind of smart delivery so you could actually make use of the data" in terms of "people, things, events, places" adding that "the more that technical infrastructure can be made to constantly reciprocate the data flows that are happening between people, formal and informal, the better." City IT staff indicated that, "the city is open to looking at doing kiosks" in support of "maps and interactive kinds of elements." Challenges were identified as "maintenance of the system" and "staff to be dedicated" to "maintaining the information." From a software engineering perspective, an academic researcher noted that "collecting data about social interactions is a challenge" as in the "open data challenge" because "social interactions can happen in many forms" giving rise to issues associated with "tracking performance."

6.6 Openness and Data for Seeing Through Smart Cities

A discussion of findings is presented in relation to the proposition under investigation in this chapter in terms of *why openness matters for data access in smart cities as data becomes more critical, complex, and valuable requiring ever more creativity associated with policy, governance, regulation, privacy, and connecting.* First, it is worth recalling the guidance by Creswell [24] that correlations in the "range from .66 to .85, "are considered very good" while those in the .35–.65 range "are useful for limited prediction." Of note, is guidance by Yin [25] who reminds us that, "case studies have been needed to examine the underlying processes that might explain a correlation."

The correlation emerging between *openness* assessed for the making of smart cities and *access to public data* when assessed as a factor contributing to the livability of smart cities considered to be very good [24] at .77. This positive correlation for *openness* and *access to public data* is evidenced in comments from city IT staff pertaining to "the desire to be very, very open with public data" and the potential for uses not "even in our mindset." The correlation emerging between *openness* assessed for the making of smart cities and *privacy* when assessed as a factor contributing to increased value for data in smart cities is considered to be useful for limited prediction [24] at .57. It is worth noting that openness is described by one individual as a feeling, as in, "a sense of freedom and openness" when associated with likable qualities of a city. The concern by Van Zoonen [15] with data-steering as control is articulated perhaps in the words of one participant where "control" issues are identified as "who owns the data, how it is housed, and the infrastructure by which it is shared" suggestive of the need for openness infrastructures and the possible privacy solution offered by Solove [22] in the form of regulating the architecture for information.

Figure 6.3 shows the correlations found between *openness* and other factors in smart cities such as *access to public data, privacy, trust,* and *connecting.*

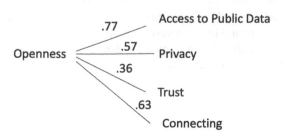

Fig. 6.3 Correlations for openness and data related factors in smart cities

The community leader who spoke of the need for "finding fun and meaningful ways to engage the public and visualize the data" and "make it about more than data" gives rise possibly to the notion of open data as "an investment in society" as advanced by Hawken et al. [2]. Additionally, this suggestion by the community leader points to the need for infrastructures that support the type of "interfaces" described perhaps by Harkins and Heard [8] in support of interactions with the "invisible that make up the data being held within our devices" and "data that is otherwise inaccessible, confusing, masked, or hidden" in response to "a growing desire to access and use this information to our benefit as a population." The potential expressed by a student for data to be "open and shared in some way that would still provide smart delivery" to "constantly reciprocate the data flows" would seem to support the recommendation by Solove [22] for architecture regulation around "the way information is used, maintained, and transferred." Continuing with the importance of play, an educator refers to the smart city as "a playful and open territory of personal and community development" as if to support the notion by Harkins and Heard [8] of "gamification" as a "method of interfacing" or interacting with "huge data sets" through "a visual platform for everyday users" pertaining to content interwoven into the life of the city.

Of note in Table 6.2 is the presence of a 25% rate of response for assessments of *access to public data* as a factor contributing to the livability of a smart city at the "neutral" position of 4. The presence of neutrality in assessment responses may be important in view of the work by Fakhrhosseini and Jeon [26] exploring emotion/ affect induction methods such as imagination where "neutral" is identified as an emotional state, among others. Nadler, Weston, and Voyles [27] also explored the use and interpretation of such midpoints in survey instruments. Infrastructure emerges in a variety of ways for openness in relation to data while issues are acknowledged associated with data access in relation to cost and affordability.

6.7   Limitations, Mitigations, and Implications

A key limitation of this chapter is the small sample size and this is mitigated by in-depth interviews with diverse individuals across multiple cities. Additionally, data were gathered systematically in parallel with this study, contributing further richness along with increased rigor from the triangulation of data. Limitations associated with elements such as geographic location and city size are mitigated by the potential to extend this study to other cities and mega-regions exceeding ten million people in size. Understanding the nature of evolving interpretations for openness in relation to data in smart cities presented challenges that are mitigated by in-depth discussions and real world examples.

6.7.1 Implications for Practice and Research

Going forward this chapter identifies implications for openness and data access pertaining to practice and research in the context of smart cities and regions.

Openness and Data: Implications for Practice

This chapter evolves openness and data challenges for practitioners in the public realm by presenting three key opportunities, as follows:

1. *Openness infrastructures.* Expanding understandings of infrastructures in support of openness that supports the interplay of human, digital/data, and physical infrastructures that are aware, interactive, and adaptive.
2. *Smarter openness.* Smart city and region initiatives involving more open mindsets in combination with more aware information architectures and more awareness of such infrastructures in support of data access, privacy, and trust.
3. *Smarter data usage.* Providing increased access opportunities for the creative, playful, and meaningful use of new data streams contributing to value for society and to more purposefulness in the public realm.

Openness and Data: Implications for Research

This chapter evolves urban theory and methods potentials for researchers by identifying three directions for future research, as follows:

1. *Openness and data.* Explore the potential of urban infrastructures for increased openness including interfaces for virtual, adaptive, and more aware interactivities.
2. *Data access, privacy, trust, and connecting.* Further exploration of data access, privacy, trust, and connecting in relation to openness in the context of more aware people and the regulating of architectures and structures underlying aware technologies, in support possibly of the notion of ambient privacy [28].
3. *Visualizing openness and Exploring other data opportunities (e.g., neutrality).* Further development, exploration, and theorizing of the openness concept focusing on real world, real time interactions, initiatives, and issues in support possibly of the notion of ambient openness [28] while exploring interpretations for neutral responses to assessments of urban elements such as *access to public data*.

In summary, challenges and opportunities for explorations of openness and data access in smart cities are presented in Table 6.8 in terms of practice and research.

Findings in terms of challenges for practice include the importance of openness and access to public data in smart cities; privacy while enabling the visualizing of urban data; and trust and openness in technology-aware environments. For research, challenges pertain to openness and urban data; openness and smart cities; and meaningful ways to engage with data in smart cities. For practice, opportunities pertain to the leveraging of openness in the city involving people; infrastructures for openness involving people; and openness in support of useful data visualizations in smart cities. For research, opportunities pertain to openness and potential uses for public data; openness to playful platforms in smart cities; and ecologies of openness involving people, data, and technologies.

This overview is intended to contribute to infrastructural improvements for openness for smart cities and regions involving elements such as those advanced by Hawken et al. [2], regarding accessibility as one of several dimensions of open data, along with interactivity and timeliness, important for real time and in the moment aspects, as well as interfaces for interactions with data aspects of the digital world as advanced by Harkins and Heard [8]. As city administration, business, community members, educators, students, and people in the city generally become more attentive to benefits of access to public data, the potential emerges for increased openness by everyone involved in relation to the development of "interfaces" and infrastructures for interacting with each other and with aware technologies in more meaningful ways, creating greater success potentials for smart cities generally and for the notion of open data and of open cities in particular.

Table 6.8 also includes key insights, patterns, spaces for dialogue, and approaches to urban theory and methods. A key insight from this chapter is the nature of the relationship between *openness and data access* and *access to public data* in smart cities where a "very good" [24] positive correlation of .77 emerged. Patterns emerging in this chapter pertained to trust as a challenge for openness where a positive correlation of .36 emerged and for privacy where a positive correlation of .57 emerged that are said to be "useful for limited prediction" [24]. Spaces for dialogue emerge in this chapter for people and privacy and trust, influencing approaches to public data openness initiatives in smart cities. Implications for urban theory and methods pertain to the potential for improving approaches to infrastructures for openness in technology-aware environments. As such, Table 6.8 serves to further support elements highlighted from the literature review in Fig. 6.1 in terms of openness infrastructures, urban openness, and interactive data and openness accommodating architectures for privacy in smart cities.

6.8 Conclusion

This chapter explores openness and data access in the context of smart cities and regions through the use of a literature review followed by a combined exploratory case study and explanatory correlational design. The significance of this chapter pertains to explorations of openness and data as yet another way of seeing through smart cities. Focusing on the smart city characteristic of openness, this chapter makes a contribution to: the smart city research literature; to urban theory in further developing understandings of data access, privacy, and openness infrastructures; and, to approaches to the study of openness and data involving assessments by

Table 6.8 Challenges & opportunities for explorations of openness and data access in smart cities

	Practice	Research
Challenges	Openness & access to public data in SCs	Openness and urban data
	Privacy & enabling visualizing of data	Openness and smart cities
	Trust and openness in tech-aware spaces	Meaningful ways to engage with data in SCs
Opportunities	Leverage openness in the city by people	Openness and potential uses for public data
	Infrastructures for openness and people	Openness to playful platforms in smart cities
	Openness and useful data visualizations	Ecologies of openness: people, data, and tech

Insights	The "very good" positive correlation between *openness* and *access to public data* in SCs
Patterns	Trust as a challenge for openness as well as privacy in tech-aware environments
Spaces for dialogue	People and privacy and trust influencing approaches to public data openness
Urban theory/ methods	Approaches to infrastructures for openness in tech-aware environments

people based on their smart city experiences. This work has implications going forward for: (a) practice, making recommendations related to: openness infrastructures; smarter openness; and smarter data usage and to (b) research, making recommendations related to: openness and data; data access, privacy, trust, and connecting; and visualizing openness and exploring other data opportunities (e.g., neutrality). A key takeaway from this work is the nature of the relationship found between *openness* and *access to public data* in smart cities as positive, with what is considered a "very good" [24] correlation of .77. While the small sample size is a key limitation of this work, the *openness* and *access to public data* finding is promising along with the *openness* and *privacy* finding with a correlation of .57, contribute to possible factors for smart cities success. This chapter also identifies spaces for dialogue in smart cities pertaining to openness infrastructures, data access, trust, and privacy. This work will be of interest to a broad audience including academics, students, city officials, business, community leaders, urban professionals and anyone concerned with smarter approaches to governance enabling smarter openness and data usage in support of smart cities and regions. As such, three questions are raised for educators, students, and community leaders, as follows:

Q 6.1. What would you say is missing from this exploration of openness as a way of seeing through smart cities? And what would your key question or questions be?
Q 6.2. How would you describe openness in a smart city or region?

Q 6.3. Is openness and data access important for smart cities and regions? Please explain briefly why or why not.

If you would like to share your responses to these questions with the author of this book an online space is provided here [https://forms.gle/Hm1HD2LygSnBd QKEA].

References

1. Gil-Garcia, J. R., Zhang, J., & Puron-Cid, G. (2016). Conceptualizing smartness in government: An integrative and multi-dimensional view. *Government Information Quarterly, 33*, 524–534. https://doi.org/10.1016/j.giq.2016.03.002
2. Hawken, S., Han, H., & Pettit, C. (Eds.). (2020). *Open cities | Open data: Collaborative cities in the information era*. Singapore: Palgrave Macmillan. https://doi.org/10.1007/978-981-13-6605-5
3. Nam, T., & Pardo, T. A. (2011). Smart city as urban innovation: Focusing on management, policy, and context. In *ICEGOV2011* (pp. 185–194).
4. Pomerantz, J., & Peek, R. (2016), Fifty shades of open. *First Monday, 21*(5). https://doi.org/10.5210/fm.v21i5.6360
5. Lehtinen, S., & Vihanninjoki, V. (2020). Seeing new in the familiar: Intensifying aesthetic engagement with the city through new location-based technologies. *Behaviour & Information Technology, 39*(6), 648–655. https://doi.org/10.1080/0144929X.2019.1677776
6. Merriam-Webster. (2020). *Access. Dictionary, thesaurus*. Retrieved August 31, 2020, from https://www.merriam-webster.com/dictionary/access
7. Merriam-Webster. (2020). *Privacy. Dictionary, thesaurus*. Retrieved September 10, 2020, from https://www.merriam-webster.com/dictionary/privacy
8. Harkins, J., & Heard, C. (2020). Interfacing the city: Mixed reality as a form of open data. In S. Hawken, H. Han, & C. Pettit (Eds.), *Open cities | Open data: Collaborative cities in the information era*. Singapore: Palgrave Macmillan.
9. Trindade Neves, F., de Castro Neto, M., & Aparicio, M. (2020). The impacts of open data initiatives on smart cities: A framework for evaluation and monitoring. *Cities, 106*, 102860. https://doi.org/10.1016/j.cities.2020.102860
10. Verhulst, S. G., & Young, A. (2017). Open data in developing economies: Toward building an evidence base on what works and how. *PB – African Minds*
11. de Waal, M., de Lange, M., & Bouw, M. (2020). The hackable city: Exploring collaborative citymaking in a network society. In K. S. Willis & A. Aurigi (Eds.), *The Routledge companion to smart cities*. London: Routledge.
12. Mattern, S. (2020, February). Post it note city: A visit to the smart city in progress at Sidewalk Toronto prompts questions about what it means to "participate" in civic design. *Places Journal*. Retrieved November 18, 2020, from https://placesjournal.org/article/post-it-note-city/
13. Lea, R. (2018). Smart cities: Technology trends (part 2). *UrbanOpus – People, Data & the Future of Cities Blog*. Retrieved November 18, 2020, from http://urbanopus.net/smart-cities-technology-trends-part-2/
14. Lea, R. (2019). The case for a smart city data brokerage. *UrbanOpus – People, Data & the Future of Cities Blog*. Retrieved November 18, 2020, from http://urbanopus.net/the-case-for-a-smart-city-data-brokerage/
15. Van Zoonen, L. (2020). Data governance and citizen participation in the digital welfare state. *Data & Policy, 2*, E10. https://doi.org/10.1017/dap.2020.10

16. Engelbert, J. (2019). Citizens, big data and ethics in the city. In *Lecture at Symposium Who Owns the City? Erasmus School of Social and Behavioural Sciences, Rotterdam, 23 January 2019.*

17. UDMS. (2020). *5th International Conference on Smart Data and Smart Cities; ISPRS; IMREDD; UCA; CNRS.* Nice, France: Urban Data Management Society. Retrieved September 13, 2020, from https://imredd.fr/en/sdsc2020/

18. Solove, D. J. (2006). A taxonomy of privacy. *University of Pennsylvania Law Review, 154*(3), 477–560. https://doi.org/10.2307/40041279

19. Van Zoonen, L. (2016). Privacy concerns in smart cities. *Government Information Quarterly, 33,* 472–480.

20. Curzon, J., Almehmadi, A., & El-Khatib, K. (2019). A survey of privacy enhancing technologies for smart cities. *Pervasive and Mobile Computing, 55,* 76–95. https://doi.org/10.1016/j.pmcj.2019.03.001

21. Stephens, T. (2020). *New data science institute includes a focus on ethics and algorithms.* NewCenter. University of California, Santa Cruz. Retrieved September 4, 2020, from https://news.ucsc.edu/2020/09/data-science-institute.html

22. Solove, D. J. (2021). The myth of the privacy paradox. *George Washington Law Review, 89* (GWU Legal Studies Research Paper No. 2020-10, GWU Law School Public Law Research Paper No. 2020-10). https://doi.org/10.2139/ssrn.3536265

23. Zaiontz, C. (2020). *Real statistics using excel.* Retrieved from www.real-statistics.com

24. Creswell, J. W. (2018). *Educational research: Planning, conducting, and evaluating quantitative and qualitative research* (6th ed.). Boston, MA: Pearson.

25. Yin, R. K. (2018). *Case study research and applications: Design and methods.* Thousand Oaks, CA: Sage.

26. Fakhrhosseini, S. M., & Jeon, M. (2017). Affect/emotion induction methods. In *Emotion and affect in human factors and human-computer interaction* (pp. 235–253). The Netherlands: Elsevier. https://doi.org/10.1016/B978-0-12-801851-4.00010-0

27. Nadler, J. T., Weston, R., & Voyles, E. C. (2015). Stuck in the middle: The use and interpretation of midpoints in items on questionnaires. *The Journal of General Psychology, 142*(2), 71–89. https://doi.org/10.1080/00221309.2014.994590

28. McKenna, H. P. (2019). *Ambient urbanities as the intersection between the IoT and IoP in smart cities.* Hershey, PA: IGI Global. https://doi.org/10.4018/978-1-5225-7882-6

Chapter 7
Innovation and Data in Smart Cities

7.1 Introduction

Gil-Garcia, Zhang, and Puron-Cid [1] identify innovation as one of several dimensions of smartness in government with an emphasis on "a new idea" and "a new practice" that "enables a government to become smarter by continuously incorporating new and improved ways to deliver services and conduct government operations." In a collection of "empirical and comparative accounts of contemporary smart cities" Karvonen, Cugurullo, and Caprotti [2] maintain that "innovation is not only *technological*" but also "involves a series of changes that are economic, sociocultural, architectural, ecological, and political." As such, the focus of this chapter is on innovation as a way of seeing and understanding smart cities.

7.2 Background

Arguing that "the wicked and tangled problems of urbanization are social, political, and organizational" Nam and Pardo [3] articulate the smart cities concept as a way for cities to innovate "in management and policy as well as technology" while taking into consideration contexts and risks. Kitchin [4] calls for a rethinking of smart cities in the form of "reframing, reimagining, and remaking" in order to "create ethical and principled" urban areas and regions "that serve all citizens." Karvonen et al. [2] highlight "the need to get inside smart cities" in order "to reveal the influence of digitialisation on broader urban dynamics." As such, the exploration of innovation and data in smart cities in this chapter gives rise to the research question:

Q1: How does *innovation* as creative opportunity contribute to value in relation to data in the public realm?

Providing additional context for this work, key terms are defined in Sect. 7.2.1.

H. P. McKenna, *Seeing Smart Cities Through a Multi-Dimensional Lens*
https://doi.org/10.1007/978-3-030-70821-4_7

7.2.1   Definitions

Definitions for key terms used in this chapter are provided based on the research literature for creativity, innovation, and data in the context of smart cities.

Creativity

Amabile [5] defines creativity as "the production of ideas or outcomes that are both novel and appropriate to some goal" which, in the case of this chapter, is the innovating of cities in the making of smarter cities.

Innovation

Amabile [5] defines innovation as "the successful implementation of creative ideas within an organization" which, in the case of this chapter, is extended across organizations in the context of cities and regions.

Collaboration, Ownership, Sharing: Data

Collaboration, ownership and sharing is described by de Waal, de Lange, and Bouw [6] using the notion of "hacking" as creative activity "at individual or collective levels" giving rise to "a sense of agency or 'ownership' in relation to a particular issue."

7.3   Innovation: A Theoretical Perspective

The innovation concept is explored and developed in this chapter through a review of the research literature in the context of smart cities and in relation to data and associated issues.

7.3.1   Innovation and Smart Cities

Ram, Cui, and Wu [7] identify five dimensions of innovation—as "something new," as "a conduit to change," as "a process'" as "a value driver," and as "invention" based on a review of the research literature. For Nam and Pardo [3], as an innovation, the smart city "harnesses the transformational potential of smart technologies" such as sensors, mobile or virtual technologies, and the like and as well, "necessitates advanced levels of sharing and integration of information and knowl-edge." Nam and Pardo [8] claim that "smart" refers to "innovative and transforma-tive changes driven by new technologies" as well as "social factors" and "policy innovation." Accordingly, Nam and Pardo [3] propose that innovation is evolution, to be understood as "a long-term strategy, not a quick solution." Also of note is the proposal by Nam and Pardo [3], that the smart city is "a harmony between the mate-rial and virtual world." Chourabi et al. [9] provide a conceptualizing of smart cities where innovation figures strongly across dimensions, in developing an integrative framework. Naphade et al. [10] identify innovation challenges for smart cities related to planning, management, and operations while claiming that "it can take a decade for a city to become truly smart." Zygiaris [11] formulates the smart city reference model consisting of several layers, one of which is the innovation layer, in support of innovation ecosystems and as a guide for "assemblies of smart planning policies." Mulder [12] focuses on public sector information (PSI) with a view to data release and reuse where co-creating "fosters further social innovation." Gascó [13] noted the absence of citizen participation when exploring "what makes a city smart" in the real world example of Barcelona as a smart city in terms of technologi-cal innovation. Citizen participation potential is then explored through "living labs as intermediaries of public open innovation" where Gascó [14] focuses on "experi-mentation in real-life contexts." Gil-Garcia, Zhang, and Puron-Cid [1] conceptual-ize smartness in government, identifying 14 dimensions, one of which is innovation and another, creativity. Gil-Garcia et al. [1] indicate that in the former case "innova-tion enables a government to become smarter" while in the latter "governments can be creative in their interventions" while promoting "an environment in which cre-ativity is encouraged." Cohen, Almirall, and Chesborough [15] speak in terms of open innovation "from open fab labs to open data" featuring cities as "a frontier for open innovation platforms for entrepreneurs, established companies, and makers" where "a vibrant public commons is needed." Urssi [16] highlights the importance for future cities of imagination in relation to information and materials. Nilssen [17] provides a typology of smart urban innovation in smart cities on a continuum of technological, organization, collaborative, and experimental. Considering artificial intelligence (AI) in terms of innovation, Kalimeri and Tjostheim [18] call for the prompt response of policymakers, regulators, and academics to concerns associated with "the invisible influence exercised by AI on human behavior" in order to "sup-port prosperity while respecting human dignity." As if building on work by Mersand, Gascó-Hernandez, Udoh, and Gil-Garcia [19] on innovative practices and digital literacies in the public library space, Ylipulli, Pouke, Luusua, and Ojala [20] advance the notion of "imagination cities" using "the case of a virtual library" referring to the notion of "the library's societal role as a portal to other realities" in order to understand "urban public spaces as hybrid spaces" involving physical spaces and virtual reality (VR) "where imagination and reality are seamlessly interlaced through VR technology." Mora et al. [21] consider urban innovation from an inter-disciplinary theoretical perspective in advancing a middle-range theory of sustain-able smart city transitions.

7.3.2   Data and Smart Cities: Collaboration, Ownership and Value

Cohen et al. [15] speak of collaboration economies, identifying the notion of "innovation ecosystems" as a role for smart cities encompassing "open fab labs to open data" for problem solving and to "generate broader entrepreneurial opportunities in the territory." It is worth recalling that de Haan, Haartsen, and Strijker [22] found that perceived success occurs "as long as citizens are continually active and in charge" of initiatives. Mosco [23] focuses on what "lies beneath" the "surface" of smart cities in a "digital world" claiming that "technology-driven smart cities deepen surveillance, shift urban governance to private companies, shrink democracy, create a hacker's paradise, and hasten the coming of catastrophic climate change." And yet, it is worth noting that de Waal et al. [6] speak of "the hackable city as a heuristic model" in terms of innovation as a way "to explore new modes of collaborative citymaking" in an emerging "network society." As such, hacking refers to "the process of clever or playful appropriation of existing technologies or infrastructures" extended to "creative practices and ideals of citymaking: spanning across spatial, social, cultural, and institutional domains." According to de Waal et al. [6], "the 'hacker' ethos" emerges "at individual or collective levels" in the form of "a sense of agency or 'ownership' in relation to a particular issue."

To remedy the "technology-driven" approach, Mosco [23] advances an approach where "people make smart cities, that human governance still matters, and that genuinely intelligent cities" begin with "a commitment to public space, and to citizen control over technology" [23]. Miller [24] describes the example of "civic hackers" in Taiwan where "the worlds of power and politics began to mix with technology and hackerdom in ways never seen before in an attempt to create a new way of making political decisions." Using the Polis platform in real time with an emergent "map showing all the different knots of agreement and dissent" and "rather than serving up the comments that were the most divisive" what is given "most visibility" is "those finding consensus" across diverse groups and no visibility is given to "divisive statement, trolling, provocation" [24]." People could "change the questions themselves" and "most valuable of all" it was found that "by clearing away the noise and divisiveness" the vTaiwan initiative "created outcomes that the government could actually act on" [24].

7.3.3   Summary

In summary, as indicated in the overview in Table 7.1, this review of the literature highlights the importance of innovation and creativity generally and in relation to data in smart cities. Organized by year from 2010 to 2020 challenges and opportunities for innovation and data are presented with Ram et al. [7] identifying dimensions of innovation; Nam and Pardo [3] highlighting the importance of policy and

Table 7.1 Overview of innovation and data in smart cities as challenges and opportunities

Author(s)	Year	Challenges	Opportunities
Ram et al.	2010	Dimensions of innovation	
Nam & Pardo	2011	Policy; sharing & integration of information & knowledge	
Naphade et al.	2011	Planning, management and operations	
Chourabi	2012	Integrative framework	
Zygiaris	2013	Assemblies of smart planning policies	
Mulder	2015	Sociable smart city	
Gascó	2016	Citizen participation & technological innovation	
Gil-Garcia et al.	2016	Innovation and smartness in government enabling creativity	
Cohen et al.	2017	Innovation ecosystems	
Gascó	2017	Living labs for real world experimentation contexts	
Urssi	2018	Imagination in relation to information & materials	
Mersand et al.	2019	Innovation practices & digital literacies	
Mosco	2019	People as critical to smart cities	
Nilssen	2019	Typology for smart urban innovation	
de Waal et al.	2020	Hacking as a heuristic model for collaborative citymaking	
Miller	2020	Social media to map consensus in real time	
Kalimeri & Tjostheim	2020	Policy on influence of AI on human behavior	
Mora et al.	2020	Theory of sustainable smart city transitions	
Ylipulli et al.	2020	Imagination cities leveraging virtual tech in public spaces	

management as well as the sharing and integration of information and knowledge; Naphade et al. [10] focusing on planning, management, and operations; Chourabi et al. [9] formulating an integrative framework for smart cities; Zygiaris [11] presents the smart city reference model to guide holistic approaches; Mulder [12] advances co-creation in support of the sociable smart city; Cohen et al. [15] identify the emergence of innovation ecosystems; Gascó [13] citizen participation and technological innovation; Gil-Garcia et al. [1] conceptualize innovation and smartness in government enabling creativity; Gascó [14] explores Living Labs as spaces for real world experimentation contexts; Urssi [16] draws attention to the importance of the imagination in relation to information and materials; Mosco [23] identifies people as critical to smart cities; Nilssen [17] develops a typology for smart urban innovation; Mersand et al. [19] identify public libraries as spaces for innovation practices and digital literacies; de Waal et al. [6] advance a heuristic model for collective citymaking where hacking is framed as a creative activity; Miller [24] describes the use of the Polis platform in Taiwan as an example of 'city hacking' for productive action and change; Kalimeri & Tjostheim [18] call for policy and regulation for artificial intelligence (AI) based on concerns with influences on human behavior; Mora et al. [21] address urban innovation through a middle-range theory of sustainable smart city transitions; and Ylipulli et al. [20] advance the notion of

Practice / Research	
Challenges	Defining urban innovation
	Innovation infrastructures
	People, imagination, and data interactions
Opportunities	Imagination and Data Value
	Innovation infrastructures
	Collaboration, Sharing, and Data visualizations

Fig. 7.1 Challenges and opportunities for innovation and data in smart cities

imagination cities using the example of virtual reality technologies in combination with public spaces such as libraries. As such, key elements this review points to the underlying and interactive elements of citizen participation, imagination, and collaborations as critical to understanding the influence of aware and emerging technologies including but not limited to artificial intelligence (AI).

Viewed another way, as depicted in Fig. 7.1, challenges and opportunities emerge for both practice and research in relation to innovation and data in everyday spaces that may also be technology embedded environments.

Challenges include defining urban innovation; innovation infrastructures; and support for people, imagination, and data interactions. Opportunities include imagination and data value; innovation infrastructures; and collaboration, sharing, and data visualizations.

7.3.4 Framework for Innovation and Data in Smart Cities

This theoretical perspective provides a background and context for development and theorizing of an innovation and data framework for smart cities and regions, operationalized for use in this chapter, as illustrated in Fig. 7.2. Through the interactive dynamic of *people—technologies—cities,* innovation as a way of seeing through smart cities is explored in relation to urban data in terms of creative opportunities, imagination, participation, collaboration, and contributing to value such as, ways to show success in real time.

The research question posed in Sect. 7.2 is reformulated here as a proposition for exploration in this chapter, as follows.

P1: *Innovation* as creative opportunity contributes to value in relation to data in the public realm in terms of potentials for smart cities such as visual ways to show success in real time.

Fig. 7.2 Conceptual
framework for innovation
and data in smart cities

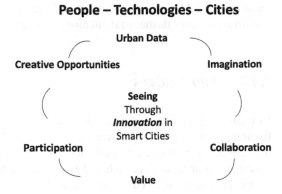

7.4 Methodology

The research design for this chapter includes an exploratory case study approach, said to be particularly appropriate for the investigation of contemporary phenomena [25], in this case, innovation and data in smart cities. Incorporating multiple methods of data collection such as survey and interview, the study underlying this chapter is combined with an explanatory correlational design [26] in support of investigating the nature of the relationship between innovation and a number of variables under study. The process, data sources, and analysis techniques for this study are described in Sects. 7.4.1–7.4.3.

7.4.1 Process

A website was used to describe the study, enable sign up, the gathering of basic demographic data, and self-identification in one or more categories (e.g., educator, student, community member, city official, business, and other). Participants were invited to complete an online survey and engage in an in-depth interview about their experience of their city or community as smart and innovative. The study attracted interest from individuals in cities in Canada, the United States, a number of European countries, and Israel.

7.4.2 Sources of Evidence

An interview protocol and a survey instrument were developed and pre-tested prior to use in the study for this chapter.

In parallel with this study, evidence was also systematically gathered from diverse voices (e.g., city officials, business, educators, students, community members, and IT staff) in a number of Canadian cities (e.g., Toronto, Vancouver, Victoria) enabling further triangulation and enriching of data.

7.4.3 Data Analysis

Content analysis was employed using a combination of deductive analysis based on findings emerging from the research literature and inductive analysis of qualitative data collected from study participants. Pattern matching, a type of content analysis was used to analyze data gathered from open ended survey questions and interviews. For quantitative data, use was made of descriptive statistics for conducting analysis of assessments made in response to survey questions. Use of the Real Statistics software add-in for Microsoft Excel [27] enabled the conducting of correlations on ordinal data from assessments for *innovation,* using *creative opportunities* as a proxy, in relation to a number of other items such as *meaningfulness* to find the Spearman correlation coefficient.

Overall, an analysis was conducted for n = 78 consisting of 41% females and 59% males for people ranging in age from their 20s to 70s.

7.5 Findings

Findings are presented in response to the research question based on an investigation of the proposition in terms of assessments for *innovation* in relation to *data use* and what people said. For example, Table 7.2 shows assessments for *innovation* using the proxy of *creative opportunities* as a factor contributing to the livability of a smart city and assessments for *innovative opportunities to make use of data* as a factor contributing to increased value for data in smart cities. On a 7-point scale, with 1 = not at all and 7 = absolutely, responses emerge for *creative opportunities* with 25% at position 3 on the scale, 50% at position 6 and 25% at position 7. Assessments for *innovative opportunities to make use of data* emerge toward the upper end of the scale with 50% at position 6 and 50% at position 7.

Table 7.3 shows assessments for *visualizing ways to show success* as a factor contributing to the success of a smart city project and assessments for *meaningfulness* as a factor contributing to increased value for data in smart cities.

Table 7.2 Assessments for innovation and innovative opportunities to make use of data

Factors	1	2	3	4	5	6	7
Creative opportunities (innovation)			25%			50%	25%
Innovative opportunities to make use of data						50%	50%

Table 7.3 Assessments for visualizing ways to show success and meaningfulness

Factors	1	2	3	4	5	6	7
Visualizing ways to show success						25%	75%
Meaningfulness						75%	25%

Table 7.4 Correlating assessments for creative opportunities and meaningfulness

Factors	Assessments	Correlation
Creative opportunities (innovation)	25% (3); 50% (6); 25% (7)	.81
Meaningfulness	75% (6); 25% (7)	

Responses emerge toward the upper end of the scale for *visualizing ways to show success* with 25% at position 6 on the scale and 75% at position 7. Assessments for *meaningfulness* emerge with 75% at position 6 and 25% at position 7.

In Table 7.4, using the Real Statistics Software add-in for Microsoft Excel [27], a correlation is conducted between *creative opportunities* as a proxy for *innovation* contributing to the livability of a smart city and *meaningfulness* as a factor contributing to increased value for data in smart cities, showing a Spearman correlation coefficient for ordinal data of .81.

Probing further, in Table 7.5, a correlation is conducted between *innovative opportunities to make use of data* as a factor contributing to increased value for data in smart cities and *visualizing ways to show success* as a factor contributing to the success of a smart city project, showing a Spearman correlation coefficient for ordinal data, of .57.

Probing further still in Table 7.6, a correlation is conducted between *innovative opportunities to make use of data* and *meaningfulness* as factors contributing to increased value for data in smart cities, showing a Spearman correlation coefficient for ordinal data of .57.

Continuing to probe, in Table 7.7 a correlation is conducted between *creative opportunities* as a proxy for *innovation* and *access to public data* as a factor contributing to the success of a smart city project, showing a Spearman correlation coefficient for ordinal data of .70.

In a survey question, when asked, "what do cities need to do to become smarter?", it is perhaps worth noting that 50% chose the option to "support smart collaboration with interactive urban displays."

Qualitatively, what follows is a glimpse of some of the things voiced by people based on their experience of a smart city in relation to innovation and data. For example, an educator pointed to the value of city apps that can "be used from ideation to real life experimentations" and "the next stages of open innovation" while "capturing the evidence of the impact." A community leader highlighted the importance of planning for "an open innovation event" enabling it to be "more engaging" with invitations to "pilot ideas" for urban challenges and opportunities. An educator and business person described examples of smartness in terms of "an advanced

Table 7.5 Correlation for innovative opportunities and visual ways to show success

Factors	Assessments	Correlation
Innovative opportunities to make use of data	50% (6); 50% (7)	.57
Visualizing ways to show success	25% (6); 75% (7)	

Table 7.6 Correlation for innovative opportunities for use of data and meaningfulness

Factors	Assessments	Correlation
Innovative opportunities to make use of data	50% (6); 50% (7)	.57
Meaningfulness	50% (6); 50% (7)	

Table 7.7 Correlation for creative opportunities and access to public data

Factors	Assessments	Correlation
Creative opportunities (innovation)	25% (3); 50% (6); 25% (7)	.70
Access to public data	50% (6); 50% (7)	

parking system" using a mobile app and "other transportation innovations." For creativity, a community leader identified the need to "move away from sector driven strategies" and "bring industries and sectors together" into "clusters" and away from "that sort of silo" approach. A building designer spoke in terms of creating a "whole urban space" where people come together "to make it feel like it is not this closed in community." In terms of smartness, a student commented that "a city becomes smart as soon as people show up with smart devices" adding that "no one wants or maybe needs a lot of visible infrastructure unless it really is 'awesome', think beautiful data visualisations in real time." This individual also stated that "a city is smart if citizen life is at the heart of all planning and integration" while highlighting the importance of meaningfulness where "smart also needs to be synonymous with social, useful, and having clear purpose." Emphasizing "the creative thinking that must come into play to innovate smarter cities" this individual stated that "people are the reason for cities and technology is only playing a bit part" where "ideas and people need to come first" with "technology to support those ideas and purposes." An educator provided a range of examples of the creative use of data in smart cities such as "smart meters for footfall, air and water quality" in addition to displays with "the number of places available in each city centre car park" as well as "real time bus data" and "one can pay for parking via mobile phones, check the shops' opening hours, etc."

7.6   Discussion: Innovation and Data for Seeing Through the City

A discussion of findings is presented for this exploration of innovation and data as a way of seeing through smart cities in terms of the proposition being explored— *Innovation* as creative opportunity contributes to value in relation to data in the public realm in terms of potentials for smart cities such as visual ways to show success in real time.

While the majority of responses for assessments of *creative opportunities* as a factor contributing to the livability of smart cities occur toward the upper end of the scale and even more so in the case of assessments of *innovative opportunities to make use of data* as a factor contributing to increased value for data in smart cities, it is important to note that 25% of responses for creative opportunities emerge toward the lower end of the scale at position 3. For some individuals it may be that creative opportunities are less important in relation to understandings of the notion of livability. In the case of *visualizing ways to show success* as a factor contributing to the success of a smart city project and *meaningfulness* as a factor contributing to increased value for data in smart cities, assessments trend toward the upper end of the scale at positions 6 and 7, with the latter slightly less so than the former.

Figure 7.3 shows the correlations found between *innovation* using *creative opportunities* as a proxy and other factors in smart cities such as *access to public data* and *meaningfulness*. *Innovative opportunities to make use of data* is also used as a proxy for *innovation* and is correlated with *visualizing ways to show success*.

In discussing the correlations that emerged, it is worth recalling the guidance by Creswell [26] that correlations in the range from .66 to .85 "are considered very good" while those in the .35–.65 range "are useful for limited prediction." Additionally, of note is guidance by Yin [25] that, "case studies have been needed to examine the underlying processes that might explain a correlation." As such, the positive correlation emerging between *creative opportunities* as a proxy for *innovation* assessed for contributing to the livability of smart cities and *meaningfulness* when assessed as a factor contributing to increased value for data in smart cities is considered to be "very good" [26] at .81 as is *access to public data* at .70. This positive correlation for *creative opportunities* and *meaningfulness* is evidenced perhaps in comments from a student pertaining to the importance of "creative thinking" and the need for smart to be "useful, and having clear purpose." Innovation and the less

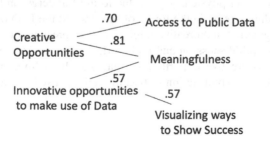

Fig. 7.3 Correlations for innovation as creative opportunities and related factors

visible are perhaps hinted at when a student refers to "beautiful data visualisations in real time" where "no one wants or maybe needs a lot of visible infrastructure unless it is really 'awesome'." The correlation emerging between *innovative opportunities to make use of data* assessed for contributing to increased value for data in smart cities and *visualizing ways to show success* when assessed as a factor contributing to the success of a smart city project is considered to be useful for limited prediction [26] at .57. This positive correlation for *innovative opportunities to make use of data* and *visualizing ways to show success* is perhaps evident in the words of an educator when speaking about the value of city apps for "ideation" for "real life experimentations" for "open innovation" and for "capturing the evidence of the impact." The correlation emerging between *innovative opportunities to make use of data* assessed for contributing to increased value for data in smart cities and *meaningfulness* when assessed as a factor contributing to increased value for data in smart cities is considered to be useful for limited prediction [26] at .57. This positive correlation for *innovative opportunities to make use of data* and *meaningfulness* gives rise possibly to the notion of innovation infrastructures and is perhaps evident in the words of a community leader regarding the need to "move away from sector driven strategies" and toward "clusters" for "industries and sectors" and through examples provided by an educator of infrastructures enabling the creative use of data in smart cities.

In summary, the notion of innovation infrastructures emerges in a variety of ways including innovation and creativity in relation to uses for data sharing while acknowledging issues associated with data collaborations in relation to silos and new forms of sharing.

7.7 Limitations, Mitigations, and Implications

A key limitation of this work is the small sample size and this is mitigated by in-depth interviews with diverse individuals across multiple cities and countries. Additionally, data gathered systematically in parallel with this study, contributes further richness along with increased rigor from the triangulation of data. Challenges associated with elements such as geographic location and city size are mitigated by the potential to extend this study to other cities and mega-regions exceeding ten million people in size. Understanding the nature of embedded and often less visible infrastructures, whether physical (e.g., in the form of underground wires and pipes and the like) or digital (e.g., in the forms of sensors and the IoT) or human (e.g., in the form of imagination and creative interactivities), presented challenges that are mitigated by in-depth discussion and real world examples. The use of proxies for innovation such as creative opportunities may also be a limitation of this work which is mitigated by exploring innovation through the use of a variety of factors.

7.7.1 Implications for Practice and Research

Going forward this work has implications for practice and research in the context of smart cities and regions.

Innovation and Data: Implications for Practice

This chapter points to challenges related to innovation and data in the public space while presenting three key opportunities for practitioners, as follows:

1. *Innovation infrastructures.* Expanding understandings of urban infrastructure to include spaces for innovation that include the potential for creativity and imagination in support of physical and digital dimensions that are aware, interactive, and adaptive.
2. *Creativity and innovation.* Urban initiatives accommodating creativity and innovation involving more aware people in combination with aware technologies extending to collaborations around the sharing and creative uses of data.
3. *Meaningful data usage.* Providing novel infrastructural supports and resources for the creative and meaningful use of new data streams enabled by sharing and collaborations contributing to the realization of data value in the public realm.

Innovation and Data: Implications for Research

This chapter evolves urban theory and methods potentials for researchers by identifying three directions for future research, as follows:

1. *Innovation and data.* Explore innovation potentials associated with more creative approaches to the sharing of data involving imaginative collaborations in relation to more meaningful and purposeful uses of data.
2. *Innovation Infrastructures.* Further exploration of the notion of innovation infrastructures for use in the study of creative behaviors involving more aware people interacting with each other and with aware technologies in smart cities and regions.
3. *Creative opportunities with a real world, real time focus.* Further development, exploration, and theorizing of the creativity concept focusing on real world, real time data interactions, initiatives, and issues in smart cities and regions.

Challenges and opportunities for explorations of innovation and data in smart cities are presented in Table 7.8 in terms of practice and research. Findings in terms of challenges for practice include the importance of partnering for innovation in smart cities; partnering in the visualizing of urban data; and collaborating for innovation as a way of seeing in smart cities. For research, challenges pertain to innovation and urban data; infrastructures for innovation in smart cities; and meaningful ways to engage with data in smart city initiatives. For practice, opportunities pertain

Table 7.8 Challenges & opportunities for explorations of innovation in smart cities

	Practice	Research
Challenges	Partnering for innovation in SCs	Innovation and urban data
	Partnering in visualizing urban data	Infrastructures for innovation in smart cities
	Collaborating for innovation as seeing	Meaningful ways to engage with data in SCs
Opportunities	Leverage city innovation by people	Innovation and potential uses for public data
	Innovation infrastructures & people	Innovation & less visible as data & infrastructure
	Innovation as seeing through SCs	Ecologies of innovation: data, people & tech

Insights	The nature of the correlation between innovation and meaningfulness as "very good"
Patterns	Positive correlations between innovation and data related factors
Spaces for dialogue	People and collaborations in relation to innovation, influencing smart city initiatives
Urban theory & methods	Influence of infrastructures for innovation in tech-aware environments

to leveraging innovation in the city involving people more meaningfully; leveraging infrastructures for innovation involving people more meaningfully; and innovation as a way of understanding and seeing through smart cities.

For research, opportunities pertain to innovation and potential uses for public data; innovation and the less visible as data and infrastructures in smart cities; and ecologies of innovation involving people, data, and technologies.

This overview is intended to contribute to infrastructural improvements for innovation for smart cities and regions that are "ethical and principled" involving the "reframing, reimagining, and remaking" advanced by Kitchin [4], in order to "serve all citizens." The sharing and using of data in useful and purposeful ways through visualizations and for informed activities and interactions in the city, in real time is suggestive perhaps of the creative activities on the individual or collective levels advanced by de Waal et al. [6].

Table 7.8 also includes key insights, patterns, spaces for dialogue, and approaches to urban theory and methods. A key insight from this chapter is the nature of the relationship between *innovation* and *meaningfulness* in terms of contributing to increased value for data in smart cities, with a positive and very good correlation. A key pattern in this chapter pertains to the consistently positive correlations between innovation and other data related factors. Spaces for dialogue emerge in this chapter for people and collaborations in relation to innovation, influencing smart city initiatives. The notion of infrastructures for innovation in support of creative interactivities has the potential for influencing urban theory and methods in technology-pervasive and aware environments. As such, Table 7.8 serves to further support elements highlighted from the literature review in Fig. 7.1 in terms of innovation infrastructures, urban innovation, imagination and data value, and interactive data and innovation accommodating more creative architectures in smart cities and regions.

7.8 Conclusion

This chapter explores innovation and data in the context of smart cities and regions through a review of the research literature and a hybrid exploratory case study and explanatory correlational design. The exploration of innovation as a way of seeing and understanding smart cities in relation to data constitutes the significance of this chapter. The main contributions of this chapter include: further development of the innovation and creativity research literature for smart cities, incorporating imagination; development and operationalization of a conceptual framework for innovation and data in smart cities; and identification of factors associated with innovation and data having the potential to influence the success of smart cities. This work has implications going forward for: (a) practice, making recommendations related to: innovation infrastructures; creativity and innovation; and meaningful data usage and (b) research, making recommendations related to: innovation and data; innovation infrastructures; and creative opportunities with a real world, real time focus.

A key take away from this work is the nature of the relationship found between *innovation* using *creative opportunities* as a proxy and *meaningfulness* with a positive and "very good" [26] correlation of .81. Although the small sample size for the study underlying this exploration is a key limitation of this chapter, the innovation and meaningfulness finding along with those for other assessments and correlations conducted (e.g., *innovative opportunities to make use of data* and *visualizing ways to show success*) also yield positive correlations. These findings, together with what people said in interviews and in response to open-ended survey questions, provide encouraging spaces for dialogue pertaining to innovation infrastructures for smart cities and regions. This chapter also points to the critical role of innovation infrastructures in support of people and creative opportunities with the potential for creating additional value by complementing the development and maintenance of existing and emergent physical, service, and digital urban infrastructures. This work will be of interest to a broad audience including academics, city officials, business, community leaders, urban professionals and anyone concerned with more creative approaches to the sharing, access, purposes, and uses of data in smart cities and regions.

As such, three questions are raised for educators, students, and community leaders, as follows:

Q 7.1. What would you say is missing from this exploration of innovation as a way of seeing through smart cities? And what would your key question or questions be?

Q 7.2. How would you describe innovation in a smart city or region?
Q 7.3. Is innovation important for smart cities and regions? Please explain briefly
    why or why not.

If you would like to share your responses to these questions with the author of
this book an online space is provided here [https://forms.gle/JZ29sCwWBfeeFP9f8].

References

1. Gil-Garcia, J. R., Zhang, J., & Puron-Cid, G. (2016). Conceptualizing smartness in government: An integrative and multi-dimensional view. *Government Information Quarterly, 33*(3),
   524–534. https://doi.org/10.1016/j.giq.2016.03.002
2. Karvonen, A., Cugurullo, F., & Caprotti, F. (2019). Introduction: Situating smart cities. In
   A. Karvonen, F. Cugurullo, & F. Caprotti (Eds.), *Inside smart cities: Place, politics and urban
   innovation* (pp. 1–12). New York, NY: Routledge.
3. Nam, T., & Pardo, T. A. (2011). Smart city as urban innovation: Focusing on management, policy, and context. In *Proceedings of the 5th International Conference on Theory and Practice of
   Electronic Governance (ICEGOV2011)* (pp. 185–194).
4. Kitchin, R. (2019). Reframing, reimagining and remaking smart cities. In C. Coletta, L. Evans,
   L. Heaphy, & R. Kitchin (Eds.), *Creating smart cities* (pp. 219–230). New York, NY:
   Routledge.
5. Amabile, T. M. (2013). Componential theory of creativity. In E. H. Kessler (Ed.), *Encyclopedia
   of management theory*. Thousand Oaks, CA: Sage.
6. de Waal, M., de Lange, M., & Bouw, M. (2020). The hackable city: Exploring collaborative
   citymaking in a network society. In K. S. Willis & A. Aurigi (Eds.), *The Routledge companion
   to smart cities*. London: Routledge.
7. Ram, J., Cui, B., & Wu, M.-L. (2010). The conceptual dimensions of innovation: A literature
   review. In *Proceedings of the International Conference on Business & Information*. Retrieved
   May 9, 2017, from http://hdl.handle.net/2440/65701
8. Nam, T., & Pardo, T. A. (2011). Conceptualizing smart city with dimensions of technology,
   people, and institutions. In *Proceedings of the 12th Annual Conference on Digital Government
   Research* (pp. 282–291).
9. Charoubi, H., Nam, T., Walker, S., Gil-Garcia, J. R., Mellouli, S., Nahon, K., ... & Scholl,
   H. J. (2012). Understanding smart cities: An integrative framework. In *Proc of the 45th HICSS*
   (pp. 2289–2297).
10. Naphade, M., Banavar, G., Harrison, C., Paraszczak, J., & Morris, R. (2011). Smarter cities and
    their innovation challenges. *Computer, 44*(6), 32–39. https://doi.org/10.1109/MC.2011.187
11. Zygiaris, S. (2013). Smart city reference model: Assisting planners to conceptualize the build-
    ing of smart city innovation ecosystems. *Journal of Knowledge Economy, 4*(2), 217–231.
12. Mulder, I. (2015). Opening up: Towards a sociable smart city. In M. Foth, M. Brynskov, &
    T. Ojala (Eds.), *Citizen's right to the digital city* (pp. 161–173). Singapore: Springer. https://
    doi.org/10.1007/978-981-287-919-6_9
13. Gascó, M. (2016). What makes a city smart? Lessons from Barcelona. In *Proceedings of the
    49th HICSS*.
14. Gascó, M. (2017). Living labs: Implementing open innovation in the public sector. *Government
    Information Quarterly, 34*, 90–98.
15. Cohen, B., Almirall, E., & Chesborough, H. (2017). The city as a lab: Open innovation meets
    the collaborative economy. *California Management Review, 59*(1), 5–13.
16. Urssi, N. J. (2018). Metacity: Design, data e urbanity. In *DUXU 2018, LNCS 10919*
    (pp. 365–378). Springer.

17. Nilssen, M. (2019). To the smart city and beyond? Developing a typology of smart urban innovation. *Technological Forecasting and Social Change, 142*, 98–104, ISSN 0040-1625. https://doi.org/10.1016/j.techfore.2018.07.060

18. Kalimeri, K., & Tjostheim, I. (2020). Artificial intelligence and concerns about the future: A case study in Norway. In N. Streitz & S. Konomi (Eds.), *HCII2020, LNCS 12203* (pp. 273–284). https://doi.org/10.1007/978-3-030-50344-4_20

19. Mersand, S., Gascó-Hernández, M., Udoh, E., & Gil-Garcia, J. R. (2019). Public libraries as anchor institutions in smart communities: Current practices and future development. In *HICSS*.

20. Ylipulli, J., Pouke, M., Luusua, A., & Ojala, T. (2020). From hybrid spaces to "imagination cities": A speculative approach to virtual reality. In K. S. Willis & A. Aurigi (Eds.), *The Routledge companion to smart cities*. London: Routledge.

21. Mora, L., Deakin, M., Zhang, X., Batty, M., de Jong, M., Santi, P., et al. (2020). Assembling sustainable smart city transitions: An interdisciplinary theoretical perspective. *Journal of Urban Technology*. https://doi.org/10.1080/10630732.2020.1834831

22. de Haan, E., Meier, S., Haartsen, T., & Strijker, D. (2018). Defining 'success' of local citizens' initiatives in maintaining public services in rural areas: A professional's perspective. *Sociologia Ruralis, 58*(2), 312–330.

23. Mosco, V. (2019). *The smart city in a digital world*. Bingley, UK: Emerald Publishing Ltd.

24. Miller, C. (2020). How Taiwan's 'civic hackers' helped find a way to run the country: New social media platform Polis cuts through noise and trolling to establish consensus—and create new laws. *The Guardian*. Retrieved September 27, 2020, from https://www.theguardian.com/world/2020/sep/27/taiwan-civic-hackers-polis-consensus-social-media-platform

25. Yin, R. K. (2018). *Case study research and applications: Design and methods*. Thousand Oaks, CA: Sage.

26. Creswell, J. W. (2018). *Educational research: Planning, conducting, and evaluating quantitative and qualitative research* (6th ed.). Boston, MA: Pearson.

27. Zaiontz, C. (2020). *Real statistics using excel*. Retrieved from www.real-statistics.com

Part III
Complexity, Disruptiveness, and Transformation in Smart Cities

Chapter 8
Disruption in Smart Cities/Regions

Navigating Pathways and Directions for Success

8.1 Introduction

Batty [1] associates disruptiveness with smart cities in posing the question—"How disruptive is the smart cities movement?" Finger [2] describes the digital layer of smart cities as having "a disruptive effect on absolutely everything" whereby, "the information contained in the data layer can be used to produce new services, new business models" and attract "new customers." Furr and Shipilov [3] argue that the notion of digital need not be disruptive and that "digital transformation" refers to "adapting an organization's structure and strategy to capture opportunities enabled by digital technology" and "more often than not, transformation means incremental steps to better deliver the core value proposition." More recently, as if in response, Batty [4] poses the question—"How disruptive are new urban technologies?" As such, the focus of this work is on an exploration of the disruptive dimension of smart cities in relation to the digital and other layers of urban environments and regions in real time, in search of patterns and relationships.

8.2 Background

Egyedi and Mehos [5] provide an understanding of disruption in the context of inverse infrastructures that "display general patterns of emergence" using the example of Wikipedia. Where traditional infrastructures "are centrally controlled by governing bodies or service providers" inverse infrastructures are said to "develop independently and outside the realm of centralized control" and are characterized as user-driven, self-organizing, having governance that is centralized and decentralized, and both top-down and bottom-up influence and decision-making, and as such, "disrupt the status quo." Borning, Friedman, and Logler [6] extend a challenge to

© Springer Nature Switzerland AG 2021
H. P. McKenna, *Seeing Smart Cities Through a Multi-Dimensional Lens*
https://doi.org/10.1007/978-3-030-70821-4_8

the information technology industry related to its participation in the ethos of "unending growth" highlighting "the constant need for novelty" along with "the accompanying throw-away culture around consumer electronics", and what is said to be "the glorification of disruption for its own sake." As such, the exploration of disruption in this chapter in relation to smart cities gives rise to the following research question:

Q1: Why is *disruptiveness* important for success in smart cities?

Providing additional context for this work, key terms are defined in Sect. 8.2.1.

8.2.1   Definitions

Definitions for key terms used in this work are provided based, in part, on the research literature for disruption and success.

Disruption

Disruption is described by Christensen, Raynor, and McDonald [7] as "a process whereby a smaller company with fewer resources is able to successfully challenge established incumbent businesses."

Disruptive Innovation

Christensen, Raynor et al. [7] indicate that when initially developed "the theory of disruptive innovation was simply a statement about correlation" where "empirical findings showed that incumbents outperformed entrants in a sustaining innovation context but underperformed in a disruptive innovation context."

Success

Christensen et al. [7] point out that "success is not built into the definition of disruption" while the Merriam-Webster Dictionary [8] defines success as "favorable or desired outcome."

8.3 Disruption: A Theoretical Perspective

The disruption concept is explored and developed through a review of the research literature in the context of smart cities and in relation to other factors including collaboration, complexity, and success. Theoretically, this work is situated at the intersection of contested challenges and opportunities for disruption and success in smart cities and regions.

8.3.1 Disruption and Smart Cities

Revisiting disruptive innovation, Christensen et al. [7] claim that considerable confusion exists about disruption theory, using the example of Uber to show that the definition does not fit since the origin of Uber was neither in a *low-end foothold* market or a *new-market foothold*. Considering Uber, Batty [1] states that "the extent to which such technologies are deeply disruptive to the form and function of the city is debatable" suggesting instead that a broader look at all the technologies taken together is needed "to figure out how all this change at so many different levels adds up to a new picture of the city and how it is evolving." Gil-Garcia, Zhang, and Puron-Cid [9] speak of cities being "resistant to disruptions" where *resiliency* as one of 14 dimensions of smartness in government is advanced. Pointing to the importance of *technology savviness*, another of 14 dimensions of smartness in government, Gil-Garcia et al. [9] note that "new and emerging technologies, over the last three decades, have continuously disrupted the administrative landscape of bureaucracies and the public sector around the world" yet, citing Gil-Garcia, Helbig, and Ojo [10], governments have been adapting to this rapid change through tool and application adoption. Focusing on the Internet of Things (IoT), Rucinski, Garbos, Jeffords, and Chowdbury [11] maintain that "the IoT impact is so profound and hard to estimate today" that it "may be categorized as 'disruptive innovation'" along with "value co-creation" as "a truly disruptive and somewhat utopian vision of collaboration."

Taylor [12] describes disruption as "a sociotechnical process involving actors, motivations, and winners and losers." Taylor [12] offers a political economy perspective on the dynamics of smart cities focusing on "disruptive urban technologies" where "the deepest disruption" is said possibly to be "that government is becoming a less important actor than its private contractors in the process of generating public-sector data" giving rise to the situation where it "increasingly risks losing access to the data that are generated." Matheri, Ngila, Njenga, Belaid, and van Rensburg [13] explore digital disruption in the energy sector claiming that "three trends converge to create game-changing disruptions"—electrification, decentralization, and digitalization. Radu [14] provides a review of the research literature where "disruptive technologies are generally considered key drivers in smart city progress" while identifying the main disruptive technologies (e.g.,

Internet of Things, big data, artificial intelligence) along with trends and challenges. More recently, Batty [4] poses the question of "how disruptive are new urban technologies?" concluding that "there are many challenges in working out the implications of how we organize old technologies as well as how we embrace new" ones. More recently, in an interview with Christensen [15] disruption is said to be "a process" and "does not mean 'breakthrough' or 'new and shiny'" or "an event" but rather, is "intertwined" with "the changing needs of customers and potential customers" and with "the constant evolution of technology."

8.3.2   Collaboration, Complexity and Success in Smart Cities

Christensen et al. [7] refer to an "intriguing anomaly" in terms of "the identification of industries that have resisted the forces of disruption" such as higher education. Christensen et al. [7] identify "online learning" as an "enabling innovation" that may "disrupt the incumbents' model" and now, with the complex challenges associated with the COVID-19 global pandemic, together with the quick response by technology developers with products such as Zoom to support online learning, meetings, conferences, and so on, at scale, the impact and role of remote working and learning would seem to be considerable. Indeed, people may be located anywhere, as in, 'digital nomads' [16] although they may be mostly at home during the pandemic, and a resituating of the notion of 'urban environments' extending to accommodate the experience of decentralization to urban regions and conurbations as people physically distance and digitally gather seems to be underway. Sterbenz [17] speaks in terms of "disruption tolerance" along with resilience for the use of the Internet of Things (IoT) in smart cities in the context of the "complex multirealm of the global Internet" as the Future Internet, where *islands and corridors of resilience* are proposed to support the interdependencies required. Taking complexity into consideration, Rzevski, Kozhevnikov, and Svitek [18] offer "an updated definition of Smart City as an Urban Ecosystem" as in, adaptive, resilient, and sustainable, that is "capable of delivering services to citizens and visitors under conditions of complexity" with "an evolutionary methodology" designed to "ensure a minimum of disruptions to city services during its transformation." Complex adaptive systems are described by Rzevski et al. [18] as exhibiting uncertain, emergent, and self-organizing behaviors in support of digital transformation to smart cities 5.0.

8.3.3   Summary

In summary, this review of the research literature provides challenges and opportunities for understandings of disruption in relation to smart cities, highlighting issues associated with collaboration, complexity, and success. As outlined in Table 8.1, an overview of disruption by author and year shows challenges and opportunities with

Table 8.1 Overview of disruption in smart cities as challenges and opportunities

Author(s)	Year	Challenges	Opportunities
Christensen et al.	2015	Understandings of disruptive innovation	
Batty	2016	Digital technologies & city form & function	
Finger	2016		Digital & Data Layer - information
Gil-Garcia et al.	2016	New & emerging technologies in government	
Rucinski et al.	2017	Disruptive innovation—IoT impact, value co-creation, collaboration, uncertainty, self-organizing	
Sterbenz	2017	Smart cities & the IoT—disruption tolerance & resilience	
Taylor	2018	Political economy perspective—risks of government as less important actor with less access to data	
Furr & Shipilov	2019		Digital transformation
Matheri et al.	2019	Energy trends & digital disruption at the grid edge	
Batty	2020	Urban technologies—organizing the old & embracing the new	
Borning et al.	2020	Glorification of disruption by IT	
Dillon	2020	Christensen on disruption as process	
Radu	2020	Disruptive technologies as drivers of smart cities	
Rzevski et al.	2020	Urban ecosystem for complex systems	

Christensen et al. [7] providing clarification on disruptive innovation; Batty [1] explores disruptiveness in smart cities in relation to technologies while calling for a broader view; Finger [2] identifies the digital and data layer of smart cities as disruptive to everything; Gil-Garcia et al. [9] point to the resiliency of smart cities and the ability for government to adapt to disruption; Rucinski et al. [11] describe the IoT as a space for disruptive innovation highlighting collaboration and value co-creation; Sternbenz [17] articulates the notion of disruption tolerance and resilience in relation to the IoT; Taylor [12] adds a sociotechnical and political economy perspective, identifying the potential risks associated with government becoming a less important actor with urban digital technologies and access to data; Furr & Shipilov [3] highlight the importance of adapting by government to digital technologies; Matheri et al. [13] explore digital disruption in the energy sector; Batty [4] looks at new urban technologies in terms of disruptiveness; Borning et al. [6] call on IT to consider issues associated with the glorification of disruption; Christensen, in an interview with Dillon [15] clarifies the intent of disruption as a process, offering theory as a tool to guide prediction; Radu [14] identifies key disruptive technologies as drivers of progress; and Rzevski et al. [18] define smart city as urban ecosystem involving adaptability, resilience, and sustainability in complex environments.

Viewed another way, as depicted in Fig. 8.1, challenges and opportunities emerge for both practice and research in relation to disruption in everyday spaces, that are associated with collaboration, complexity, and success in smart cities.

Challenges for practice and research include defining urban disruption; disruption infrastructures or inverse infrastructures; and adaptability, resilience, and

Practice / Research	
Challenges	Defining urban disruption
	Disruption infrastructures
	Adaptability, resilience, and sustainability
Opportunities	Disruption and Adaptability
	Disruption infrastructures
	Collaboration, Complexity, and Success

Fig. 8.1 Challenges and opportunities for disruption in smart cities

sustainability. Opportunities include disruption and adaptability; disruption infra-structures; and collaboration, complexity, and success. Additionally, this review of the literature points to the underlying and interactive elements of uncertainty, self-organizing, and emergent behaviors as critical to working with disruption in complex urban environments and regions.

8.3.4   Conceptual Framework for Disruption and Smart Cities

This theoretical perspective provides a background and context for the formulation, development, and operationalization of a framework for disruption and smart cities. As illustrated in Fig. 8.2, through the interactive dynamic of *people—technologies—cities,* disruption as a way of seeing through smart cities is explored in relation to urban data in terms of adapting for urban uses, cross-sector collaborations, and visual ways to show success in real time, including data to inform, educate, and inspire while contributing to understandings of success in contemporary urban environments and regions.

The research question posed in Sect. 8.2 is reformulated here as a proposition for exploration in this paper, as follows.

P1: *Disruptiveness* is important for success in smart cities, associated as it is with opportunities for adaptiveness, collaborations, and the use of data to inform, educate, and inspire in real time.

8.4   Methodology

The research design for this work included an exploratory case study approach, important as it is for the study of contemporary phenomena [19], incorporating multiple methods of data collection including interview and survey, combined with

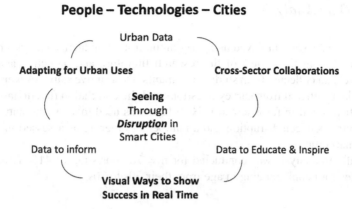

Fig. 8.2 Conceptual framework for disruption and smart cities

an explanatory correlational design to investigate the relationship between variables [20]. Yin [19] advises that, "case studies have been needed to examine the underlying processes that might explain a correlation." The process, data sources, and analysis techniques for the study underlying this chapter are described in Sects. 8.4.1–8.4.3.

8.4.1   Process

A website was used to describe the study, enable sign up, the gathering of basic demographic data, and self-identification in one or more categories (e.g., educator, student, community member, city official, business, and other). Participants were invited to complete an online survey and engage in an in-depth discussion of their experience of their city or community as smart, along with disruptive factors. The study attracted interest from individuals in cities in Canada, the United States, a variety of European countries, and Israel.

8.4.2   Sources of Evidence

An interview protocol and a survey instrument were developed and pre-tested prior to use in the study. In parallel with this study, data were systematically gathered from diverse voices (e.g., city officials, business, educators, students, community members, and IT staff) in small to medium to large-sized Canadian cities (e.g., Toronto, Vancouver, Victoria) enabling further triangulation and enriching of data.

8.4.3   Data Analysis

Content analysis was employed using a combination of deductive analysis based on terminology from the review of the research literature and inductive analysis of qualitative data collected from study participants. Descriptive statistics were used to analyze data gathered from survey questions and the correlation functionality in the Real Statistics add-in for Microsoft Excel [21] was used to show the nature of the relationships between disruption and a number of other items assessed in the context of smart cities.

Overall, an analysis was conducted for n = 78 consisting of 41% females and 59% males for people ranging in age from their 20s to 70s.

8.5   Findings

Findings are presented in response to the research question based on an exploration of the proposition in terms of disruption and a variety of items assessed—*cross-sector collaborations*; *visualizations of data to inform, educate, and inspire in real time;* and *visual ways to show success in real time*—and what people said in coming to new understandings of the challenges, opportunities, and potentials for *disruption* as a way of seeing through smart cities.

Table 8.2 shows survey responses for *adapting for urban uses* as a proxy for *disruption*, when asked to assess city-focused social media and other aware technologies as giving rise to many possibilities. On a 7-point scale where 1 = not at all and 7 = absolutely, 25% responded at position 5, 25% at position 6 and 50% at position 7.

As shown in Table 8.3, when asked to assess factors contributing to the success of a smart city project, on a 7-point scale where 1 = not at all and 7 = absolutely, in response to *cross-sector collaborations*, 50% responded at position 6 and 50% at position 7.

Using the Real Statistics Software add-in for Microsoft Excel [21], a correlation is conducted between *adapting for urban uses* as a proxy for *disruption* when assessing city-focused social media and other aware technologies as giving rise to many possibilities and *cross sector-collaborations* as a factor contributing to the

Table 8.2 Disruption assessments as an element contributing to the making of smart cities

Variables	1	2	3	4	5	6	7
Adapting for urban uses (disruption)					25%	25%	50%

Table 8.3 Cross-sector collaboration assessed as contributing to the success of a SC project

Variables	1	2	3	4	5	6	7
Cross-sector collaborations						50%	50%

Table 8.4 Correlating assessments for disruption and cross-sector collaborations

Items	Assessments	Correlation
Adapting for urban uses (disruption)	25% (5); 25% (6); 50% (7)	.94
Cross-sector collaborations	50% (6); 50% (7)	

Table 8.5 Correlating assessments for disruption and visualizations (data value)

Items	Assessments	Correlation
Adapting for urban uses (disruption)	25% (5); 25% (6); 50% (7)	.54
Visualizations of data inform-educate-inspire	75% (6); 25% (7)	

success of a smart city project, showing a positive Spearman correlation coefficient for ordinal data in Table 8.4, of .94.

Probing further, as shown in Table 8.5, when asked to assess the extent to which *visualizations of data that inform, educate, and inspire in real time* contribute to increased value for data in smart cities, 75% responded toward the upper end of the scale at position 6 and 25% at position 7. When *disruption* using *adapting for urban uses* as a proxy is correlated with *visualizations of data that inform, educate, and inspire in real time*, a positive Spearman correlation coefficient emerges of .54.

Probing further still, as shown in Table 8.6, when asked to assess the extent to which *visual ways to show success in real time* contribute to the success of a smart city project, 75% responded at the upper end of the scale at position 7 and 25% at position 6. When *disruption* using *adapting for urban uses* as a proxy is correlated with *visual ways to show success in real time*, a positive Spearman correlation coefficient of .27 emerges.

Continuing to probe, as shown in Table 8.7, assessments of *cross-sector collaborations* are correlated with those for *visualizations of data that inform, educate, and inspire in real time* showing a positive Spearman correlation coefficient of .57.

Survey responses also indicated that when asked what cities need to do to become smarter, people unanimously (100%) selected the option to "make engagement smarter (e.g., break down the silos and collaborate more)" and the option to "make participation smarter (e.g., remove the red tape and bureaucracy)" while 50% selected the option to "support smarter collaboration with interactive urban displays." In smart city discussions, a community leader stressed the need to move toward "clusters" for "industries and sectors" to come together "rather than that sort of silo" thinking.

An urban education innovator pointed to the challenge of an "uncertain future" and as if in demonstration of such uncertainty, during the writing of this book, the emergence of the COVID-19 global pandemic occurred, spreading quickly around the world, disrupting everything about life as we know it, including all manner of interactions and activities in cities and regions. A student commented that "post pandemic we are discovering that many office jobs can be done from home" possibly rendering "office blocks a thing of the past." An individual in the information

Table 8.6 Correlating disruption assessments and visual ways to show success

Items	Assessments	Correlation
Adapting for urban uses (disruption)	25% (5); 25% (6); 50% (7)	.27
Visual ways to show success in real time	25% (6); 75% (7)	

Table 8.7 Correlating assessments for cross-sector collaborations and data visualizations

Items	Assessments	Correlation
Cross-sector collaborations	50% (6); 50% (7)	.57
Visualizations of data inform-educate-inspire	75% (6); 25% (7)	

technology sector provided Uber as a "perfect example" of inverse infrastructures, providing "bottom up" taxi service that is "non-licensed" with "no official screening process" where "we watch technology kind of take over and it just becomes a social engineered thing." An urban public engagement consultant provided the example of little free libraries as "pocket spaces" around the community where things in the form of books were described, to illustrate "there is human interaction," along with mapping to show location which incorporates the use of "technology and the space" all of which become parts of an emergent and inverse-like infrastructure.

Regarding complexity, an IT developer providing services to municipal governments and postsecondary institutions observed that there are "a lot of moving pieces to make a smart city" such that, "implementation is going to be the biggest challenge" because "everything about it would have to be dynamic, down to managing the different departments." Highlighting the process nature of cities, City IT staff acknowledged that "we're using tools to manage processes but we're not using them to the fullest extent." Regarding success, City IT added that with "more rich, accurate data in the tools, publishing that data" and "using different tools to interrogate and present data becomes that much more important and it contributes to how we successfully engage with the citizenry around those elements."

The example of an eTownHall meeting was provided "because we've brought technology" to the space enabling "bringing questions in and sharing answers through Twitter" and other social media, enabling "another level of engagement that our Citizen Engagement Department was very interested in because it gave them a dataset that was above and beyond" the usual, in the form of "documented engagement." A community member pointed to the importance of "using data from technologies to improve aspects of the city" adding that "the human component" is critical "in order to enable all those connections." A student identified "data visualizations rather than just urban displays" as important for "getting people involved." Referring to "city dashboards" a student suggested that "you can take these bits of data and rather than present numbers you can make beautiful artistic visualizations." City IT staff indicated that they are "in the process of designing a citizen portal" enabling people to enter an interactive space "personalized for them." A community member suggested the need for "not too dense information on what's happening at a particular point so that you can access this type of information and know what's going on in real time almost" using the example of cellphone parking lots at airports and the smartness aspect that "decreases congestion." Thinking about emerging technologies in the city, an educator suggested that "it's the act of engaging with the artifacts" so that "it's the interaction with the object and what the object affords us" and "they do become affordances in society," raising the question of "how do you engage with that space?" A community member noted that "creating a more engaged citizenry" involving the use of "technology and social media working together" could be realized in relation to discussion on urban issues such as a "development proposal" since it "affects everybody because their environment is being changed." An urban public engagement consultant spoke of "digital engagement" and "the apps and engagement tools" as a mechanism "to encourage people to do some observations of space and people."

8.6 Discussion: Disruption and Seeing Through Smart Cities

A discussion of findings is presented for this exploration of disruption as a way of seeing through smart cities in terms of the proposition being explored where *disruption* as *adapting for urban uses* and other factors such as *cross-sector collaborations* contributes to success in the public realm in terms of potentials for smart cities such as *the use of data to inform, educate, and inspire in real time*.

The strong support (100%) provided from survey responses for the option to "make engagement smarter (e.g., break down the silos and collaborate more)" is important because engagement is said to be key for smart city success [22]. This is also evident in the words of a community leader who spoke of collaboration in terms of "clusters" for "industries and sectors" as a way of coming together and moving beyond "silo" thinking. The lower selection rate of 50% for the option to "support smarter collaboration with interactive urban displays" is interesting to consider in view of the suggestion by a student highlighting the need for "data visualizations rather than just urban displays" for "getting people involved." It may also be that the evolving of urban displays to incorporate more interactive elements is needed in support of collaboration, engagement, and participation.

Adapting and Collaborations While responses tended toward the upper end of the scale for assessments of *disruption* employing the proxy of *adapting for urban uses* as a factor giving rise to many possibilities for the use of city-focused social media and other aware technologies in smart cities, responses were even higher in the case of assessments of *cross-sector collaborations* as a factor contributing to the success of a smart city project. However, when correlated, a Spearman correlation for ordinal data of .94 emerged and it is worth recalling the guidance by Creswell [20] that "when two or more variables are related, correlations this high are seldom achieved" as in, the "range from .86 and above" and that "two variables actually

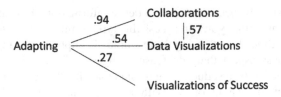

Fig. 8.3 Correlations for disruption as adapting and related factors in smart cities

measure the same underlying trait and should probably be combined in data analysis." Figure 8.3 shows the correlations found between *disruption* using *adapting for urban uses* as a proxy and other factors in smart cities such as *cross-sector collaborations* (.94), *visualizations of data to inform, educate, and inspire in real time*, (.54) and *visual ways to show success in real time* (.27).

Adapting and Data Visualizations For *visualizations of data to inform, educate, and inspire in real time* as a factor contributing to the success of a smart city project, assessments also trend toward the upper end of the scale at positions 6 and mostly at position 7. When correlated with *adapting for urban* uses, a Spearman correlation of .54 emerges and, according to Creswell [20], correlations in the .35–.65 range "are useful for limited prediction." This positive correlation for *disruption* using the *adapting for urban uses* as a proxy and *visualizations of data to inform, educate, and inspire in real time* is perhaps evident in the comments by city IT that "we're using tools to manage processes but we're not using them to the fullest extent" to "present data" and as this evolves, potential exists for this correlation to change and become stronger, influencing for example, smart city success.

Collaborations and Data Visualizations When *visualizations of data to inform, educate, and inspire in real time* is correlated with *cross-sector collaborations*, a slightly stronger correlation of .57 emerges. This positive correlation for *cross-sector collaborations* and *visualizations of data to inform, educate, and inspire in real time* emerges perhaps in the description by an urban public engagement consultant of little free libraries with "human interaction" on the community level featuring the collaborative sharing of books along with technology to map the many library locations as a kind of data visualization to inform, with books as things to educate and inspire.

Adapting and Visualizations of Success Exploring for further relationships, *visual ways to show success in real time* as another factor contributing to the success of a smart city project was also assessed toward the upper end of the scale and when correlated with *adapting for urban uses* shows a Spearman correlation of .27 which according to Creswell [20], for correlations in the .20–.35 range "there is only a slight relationship." Again, this positive correlation is perhaps evident in the description of little free libraries as a type of *adapting for urban uses* and as a form of resilience, together with the not so visible infrastructure, gives rise possibly to the notion of inverse infrastructures for sharing and success in real time.

In summary, the notion of adaptability and uncertainty [18] in disruptive environments emerges in a variety of ways including *adapting for urban uses* in relation to visualizing data and collaboration potentials while acknowledging issues associated with engagement in relation to silos and new forms of collaboration across sectors.

8.7 Limitations, Mitigations and Implications

A key limitation of this work is the small sample size and this was mitigated by in-depth interviews from diverse individuals across multiple cities. The use of proxies for *disruption* such as *adapting for urban uses* may also be a limitation of this work which is mitigated by exploring disruption in variety of ways. Additionally, data were gathered systematically in parallel with this study, contributing further richness along with increased rigor from the triangulation of data. Challenges associated with elements such as geographic location and city size were mitigated by the potential to extend this study to other cities and mega-regions exceeding ten million people in size. Understanding the nature of possibly less visible aspects of disruption presented challenges that were mitigated by in-depth discussion and real world examples.

8.7.1 Implications for Practice and Research

Going forward this chapter has implications for practice and research in the context of disruption and smart cities and regions in a variety of ways.

Disruption and Smart Cities: Implications for Practice

From the range of challenges for practitioners in smart cities and regions pertaining to disruption that are identified in this chapter, three key opportunities for navigating pathways and directions for success are presented here, as follows:

1. *Adapting for Urban Uses.* Expanding understandings of disruption to adaptability, as in, adapting for urban uses as a way of responding to, participating in, becoming resilient through, and becoming involved in smart city initiatives.
2. *Cross-sector Collaborations.* Disrupting siloed thinking through the creation of novel, unlikely, and productive collaborations in smart city initiatives.
3. *Data Visualizations in Real Time.* Leveraging public data in real time to educate, inform, and inspire through collaborative smart city initiatives.

Disruption and Smart Cities: Implications for Research

From the range of challenges pertaining to disruption that are identified in this chapter for researchers in smart cities and regions, three opportunities for navigating pathways and directions for success for future research are presented here, as follows:

1. *Adaptability and Collaborations in Complex Environments.* Extending complexity theory to incorporate adaptability in combination with collaborations in real time urban environments and regions.
2. *Visual Ways to Show Success in Real Time.* Extending data visualizations to show factors contributing to success in real time in smart cities and regions, such as more and smarter engagement, as articulated perhaps by Gardner and Hespanhol [23].
3. *Inverse Infrastructures, Resilience, and Uncertainties in Real Time.* Extending understandings of smart cities showing how potentially disruptive developments such as the introduction of inverse infrastructures may also contribute to resilience and the capability to respond to uncertainties in real time.

Challenges and opportunities for explorations of disruption in smart cities are presented in Table 8.8 in terms of practice and research. Findings in terms of challenges for practice include the importance of collaborating across sectors in smart cities; collaborating in the visualizing of urban data; and disruption as a way of seeing through smart cities.

Table 8.8 Challenges & opportunities for explorations of disruption in smart cities

	Practice	Research
Challenges	Collaborating and disruption in SCs	Disruption and urban data
	Collaborating in visualizing urban data	Disruption and smart cities
	Disruption as seeing through smart cities	Engagement in smart city initiatives
Opportunities	Adaptability & disruption by people	Disruption and potential uses for public data
	Infrastructures & disruption by people	Disruption and inverse infrastructures in SCs
	Disruption & resilience in smart cities	Disruption: people, data, and tech

Insights	The relationship between disruption and visualizations of data to inform-educate-inspire
Patterns	The positive correlations between disruption and other data visualizations in smart cities
Spaces for dialogue	People collaborating as an element of disruption, influencing smart city success
Urban theory/ methods	Visualizations of data to inform and influence in tech-aware environments

For research, challenges pertain to understanding disruption and urban data; disruption and smart cities; and engagement in smart city initiatives. For practice, opportunities pertain to adaptability in relation to disruption in the city involving people; infrastructures supporting disruption involving people; and disruption and resilience in smart cities. For research, opportunities pertain to disruption and potential uses for public data; disruption and inverse infrastructures in smart cities; and disruption involving people, data, and technologies.

Table 8.8 also includes key insights, patterns, spaces for dialogue, and elements relevant to urban theory and methods. A key insight from this chapter is the nature of the relationship between disruption and visualizations of date to inform, educate and inspire in real time with a positive correlation (.54) in smart cities. A key pattern emerging in this chapter is the presence of positive correlations between proxies for disruption (e.g., adapting for urban uses, cross-sector collaborations) and other data visualizations in smart cities. Spaces for dialogue emerge in this chapter in terms of people collaborating across sectors as an element of disruption, influencing the potential for success of smart city initiatives extending possibly to approaches in support of visualizations of data to inform, educate, and inspire in real time influencing urban theory and methods in technology-pervasive and aware environments. As such, Table 8.8 serves to further support elements highlighted from the literature review in Fig. 8.1 in terms of infrastructures that support disruption and adaptability; defining and understanding urban disruption; and collaboration, complexity and success in smart cities and regions.

8.8 Conclusion

This chapter explores disruption in smart cities and regions through a literature review and then a case study combined with an explanatory correlational design investigating factors pertaining to assessments for data visualizations. Focusing on the potential for disruption to serve as a way of seeing and understanding smart cities, this chapter makes a contribution in a number of ways, as follows: a review of the research literature exploring disruption, in relation to smart cities is provided; development and operationalization of a conceptual framework for disruption and smart cities; and correlations are provided for disruption (using *adapting for urban uses* as a proxy) in relation to a variety of factors based on assessments by people and their experiences of smart cities. This work has implications going forward for: (a) practice, making recommendations related to: adapting for urban uses, cross-sector collaborations, and data visualizations in real time and for (b) research, making recommendations related to: adaptability and collaborations in complex environments; visual ways to show success in real time; and inverse infrastructures, resilience, and uncertainties in real time. A key take away from this work is the critical role of people and their generation of human infrastructures and possibly inverse infrastructures in adapting to disruption in urban environments, contributing to the potential for success, whether through data visualizations or leveraging data for urban purposes This chapter will be of interest to a broad audience including academics, students, city officials, business, community leaders, urban professionals and anyone concerned with the challenges and opportunities associated with disruption while navigating pathways and directions for success in the context of smart cities and regions. As such, three questions are raised for educators, students, and community leaders, as follows:

Q 8.1. What would you say is missing from this exploration of disruption as a way of seeing through smart cities? And what would your key question or questions be?

Q 8.2. How would you describe disruption in a smart city or region?

Q 8.3. Is disruption important for smart cities and regions? Please explain briefly why or why not.

If you would like to share your responses to these questions with the author of this book an online space is provided here [https://forms.gle/nmTC8gaMsrt NT5j19].

References

1. Batty, M. (2016). How disruptive is the smart cities movement? Editorial. *Environment and Planning B: Planning and Design, 43*(3), 441–443. https://doi.org/10.1177/0265813516645965
2. Finger, M. (2016). *Smart cities—Management of smart urban infrastructures. (Massive Open Online Course)*. Lausanne, Switzerland: École Polytechnique Fédérale de Lausanne.
3. Furr, N., & Shipilov, A. (2019, July–August). Digital doesn't have to be disruptive. *Harvard Business Review.*
4. Batty, M. (2020). How disruptive are new urban technologies? Editorial. *Urban Analytics and City Science Environment and Planning B (EPB), 47*(1), 3–6. https://doi.org/10.1177/2399808320902574
5. Egyedi, T. M., & Mehos, D. C. (Eds.). (2012). *Inverse infrastructures: Disrupting networks from below.* Cheltenham, UK: Edward Elgar Pub. https://doi.org/10.4337/9781781952290
6. Borning, A., Friedman, B., & Logler, N. (2020). The 'invisible' materiality of information technology. *Communications of the ACM, 63*(6), 57–64.
7. Christensen, C. M., Raynor, M. E., & McDonald, R. (2015, December). What is disruptive innovation? *Harvard Business Review.* Retrieved September 29, 2020, from https://hbr.org/2015/12/what-is-disruptive-innovation
8. Merriam-Webster. (2020). *Success. Dictionary, thesaurus.* Retrieved October 11, 2020, from https://www.merriam-webster.com/dictionary/success
9. Gil-Garcia, J. R., Zhang, J., & Puron-Cid, G. (2016). Conceptualizing smartness in government: An integrative and multi-dimensional view. *Government Information Quarterly, 33*(3), 524–534. https://doi.org/10.1016/j.giq.2016.03.002
10. Gil-Garcia, J. R., Helbig, N., & Ojo, A. (2014). Being smart: Emerging technologies and innovation in the public sector. *Government Information Quarterly, 31*, I1–I8.
11. Rucinski, A., Garbos, R., Jeffords, J., & Chowdbury, S. (2017). Disruptive innovation in the era of global cyber-society: With focus on smart city efforts. In *Proceedings of the 9th IEEE International Conference on Intelligent Data Acquisitions and Advanced Computing Systems: Technology and Applications.*

12. Taylor, L. (2018). What can 'disruptive urban technologies' tell us about power, visibility and the right to the city? *International Journal of Urban and Regional Research (IJURR)*, 42
13. Matheri, A. N., Ngila, J. C., Njenga, C. K., Belaid, M., & van Rensburg, N. J. (2019). Smart city energy trend transformation in the fourth industrial revolution digital disruption. In IEEE *International Conference on Industrial Engineering and Engineering Management (IEEM), Macao, China, 2019* (pp. 978–984). https://doi.org/10.1109/IEEM44572.2019.8978675
14. Radu, L.-D. (2020). Disruptive technologies in smart cities: A survey on current trends and challenges. *Smart Cities, 3*, 1022–1038. https://doi.org/10.2290/smartcities3030051
15. Dillon, K. (2020, February 4). Disruption 2020: An interview with Clayton M. Christensen. *MIT Sloan Management Review*. Retrieved October 11, 2020, from https://sloanreview.mit.edu/article/an-interview-with-clayton-m-christensen/?og=Disruption+2020+Horizontal
16. Wang, B., Schlagwein, D., Cecez-Kecmanovic, D., & Cahalane, M. C. (2018). Digital work and high-tech wanderers: Three theoretical framings and a research agenda for digital nomadism. In *ACIS 2018 Proceedings* (p. 55). Retrieved from https://aisel.aisnet.org/acis2018/55
17. Sterbenz, J. P. G. (2017). Smart city and IoT resilience, survivability, and disruption tolerance: Challenges, modelling, and survey of research opportunities. In *9th International Workshop on Resilient Networks Design and Modeling (RNDM), Alghero* (pp. 1–6). https://doi.org/10.1109/RNDM.2017.8093025
18. Rzevski, G., Kozhevnikov, S., & Svitek, M. (2020). Smart city as an urban ecosystem. In *2020 Smart City Symposium Prague (SCSP), Prague, Czech Republic, 2020* (pp. 1–7). https://doi.org/10.1109/SCSP49987.2020.9133849
19. Yin, R. K. (2018). *Case study research and applications: Design and methods*. Thousand Oaks, CA: Sage.
20. Creswell, J. W. (2018). *Educational research: Planning, conducting, and evaluating quantitative and qualitative research* (6th ed.). Boston, MA: Pearson.
21. Zaiontz, C. (2020). *Real statistics using excel*. Retrieved from www.real-statistics.com
22. SmartCitiesWorld. (2018). Citizen engagement is key to smart city success. *SmartCitiesWorld*. Retrieved October 12, 2020, from https://www.smartcitiesworld.net/news/news/citizen-engagement-is-key-to-smart-city-success-2685
23. Gardner, N., & Hespanhol, L. (2018). SMLXL: Scaling the smart city, from metropolis to individual. *City, Culture and Society, 12*, 54–61. https://doi.org/10.1016/j.ccs.2017.06.006

Chapter 9
After Synthesizing and Analyzing

A Typology for Seeing Through Smart Cities

9.1 Introduction

This chapter provides a synthesis of the preceding chapters in this book, offering potentials for seeing through the lens of smart cities, across a range of dimensions and perspectives. An overview is provided of the literature reviews conducted, chapter-by-chapter focusing on multiple dimensions for seeing through smart cities as—sensing, awareness, learning, openness, innovation, and disruption. Keeping in mind the guidance by Naphade et al. [1] in Chap. 7 that "it can take a decade for a city to become truly smart" this work is also attentive to the perspective provided in Chap. 8 that disruptive innovation is a process, according to Christensen [2], contributing to transformation [1] as technologies evolve and as people and their needs change [2]. An overview and analysis of results from the hybrid approach to seeing through smart cities and regions that was used in this work is then provided, consisting of findings from the combining of an exploratory case study with an explanatory correlational design.

Objective The primary objective of this chapter is to provide a synthesis of this book contributing to an overview of perspectives, relationships, and patterns for identifying directions and pathways for increasing success in smart cities and regions.

9.2 Seeing Through the Lens of Smart Cities

This section revisits the conceptual framework for seeing smart cities through a multi-dimensional lens developed in Chap. 1, providing: a componential view of the explorations conducted throughout this book, an overview of the theoretical perspective, and an overview of challenges and opportunities emerging from the literature reviews.

© Springer Nature Switzerland AG 2021
H. P. McKenna, *Seeing Smart Cities Through a Multi-Dimensional Lens*
https://doi.org/10.1007/978-3-030-70821-4_9

9.2.1   Seeing Through Smart Cities: Taking Another Look

While Chap. 1 presented a conceptual framework for seeing smart cities through a multi-dimensional lens and Chap. 3 provided a revised framework to accommodate a hybrid exploratory and explanatory research design, this chapter again revisits the framework, providing an opportunity to reflect on operationalization of the framework in this book in light of discussions with diverse individuals in multiple cities in multiple countries in the context of smart cities and regions. As illustrated in Fig. 9.1, through the interactive dynamic of *people—technologies—cities,* the constructs of awareness, sensing, learning, openness, innovation, and disruption are investigated in this book as key dimensions of smart cities using an exploratory case study combined with an explanatory correlational design, contributing to emergent understandings and insights. The terms "Perspectives" and "Patterns" are added to the left portion of the image based on case study explorations; the term "Relationships" appears in the right portion of the image based on explanatory correlations; while at the bottom of the image, the terms "Experiences" and "Interpretations" are added based on case study findings.

What follows is an enriching of this framework through a componential view of the contents explored in this book.

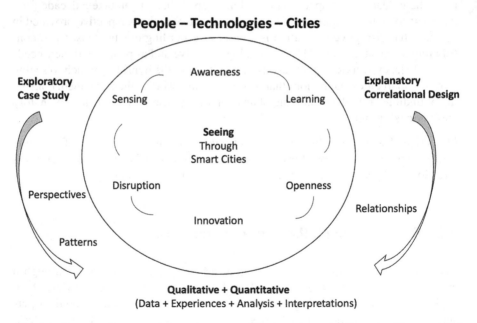

Fig. 9.1 Conceptual framework for seeing smart cities through a multi-dimensional lens revisited

9.2.2 Seeing Through Smart Cities: A Componential View

Table 9.1 provides an overview of the component conceptual frameworks developed and operationalized in this book, chapter-by-chapter in support of dimensions identified in Fig. 9.1. Each of the six dimensions explored in this book—sensing, awareness, learning, openness, innovation, and disruption—form components of seeing through smart cities, consisting in turn of elements that form the conceptual framework for each. As shown in Table 9.1, for the *sensing* dimension, the conceptual framework for sensing by people in smart cities consists of the elements of attuning to urban spaces, emotion/affect in the form of comfort, and both visible and less visible infrastructures.

For the *awareness* dimension, the conceptual framework for awareness in smart cities consists of the elements of ICTs, access to public data, privacy, and trust. For the *learning* dimension, the conceptual framework for learning and data in smart cities consists of the elements of learning infrastructures, knowledge and data infrastructures, privacy, trust, and security. For the *openness* dimension, the conceptual framework for openness in smart cities consists of the elements of urban data, access, privacy, governance, connecting, and trust. For the *innovation* dimension, the conceptual framework for innovation and data in smart cities consists of the elements of urban data, collaboration, imagination, participation, and value. For the *disruption* dimension, the conceptual framework for disruption and smart cities consists of the elements of cross-sector collaborations, visualizations of data that inform, educate, and inspire in real time; and visual ways to show success in real time.

These conceptual frameworks emerged from a review of the research literature for each of the six dimensions, as described in Sect. 9.2.3.

Table 9.1 Componential conceptual frameworks for seeing through smart cities

Dimensions	Componential conceptual frameworks
Sensing	Conceptual framework for sensing by people in smart cities *Attuning–emotion/affect (comfort)—infrastructure: visible/less visible*
Awareness	Conceptual framework for awareness in smart cities *ICTs—access to public data—privacy—trust*
Learning	Conceptual framework for learning and data in smart cities *Infrastructures (learning—knowledge & data)—privacy—trust—security*
Openness	Conceptual framework for openness in smart cities *Urban data—access—privacy—governance—connecting—trust*
Innovation	Conceptual framework for innovation and data in smart cities *Urban data—collaboration—imagination—participation—value*
Disruption	Conceptual framework for disruption and smart cities *Cross-sector collaborations—data to inform—visual ways to show success*

9.2.3   Seeing Through Smart Cities: Theoretical Perspectives

In developing a theoretical perspective for this work, an overview of the research literature explored in each chapter is presented in Table 9.2. Chapter 1 focuses on developing a lens for seeing through smart cities based on a review of the research literature for emerging technologies and smart cities; urban theory and smart cities; people and smart cities; and the disruptive and contested nature of smart city initiatives. Chapter 2 focuses on sensing as spaces for people through a review of the research literature for sensing and smart cities; spaces for people and smart cities; agency and smart cities; and emotion/affect and smart cities. Chapter 3 introduces the rationale for a hybrid exploratory case study and correlational explanatory design approach applied to findings for Chapter 2 and as a model for subsequent chapters. Chapter 4 focuses on awareness as seeing, through a review of the research literature for awareness, people, and smart cities; and then for ICTs, urban data, and smart cities. Chapter 5 focuses on learning and data in smart cities through a review of the research literature for learning and smart cities; and then for data and smart

Table 9.2 Theoretical perspectives for seeing through smart cities

Chapter	Theoretical perspectives
Chapter 1	Seeing through smart cities – Emerging technologies and smart cities – Urban theory and smart cities – People and smart cities – Disruptive and contested nature of smart city initiatives
Chapter 2	Sensing as spaces for people – Sensing and smart cities – Spaces for people and smart cities – Agency and smart cities – Emotion/affect and smart cities
Chapter 3	(Methodological approach)
Chapter 4	Awareness as seeing – Awareness, people, and smart cities – ICTs, urban data, and smart cities
Chapter 5	Learning and data in smart cities – Learning and smart cities – Data and smart cities
Chapter 6	Openness and data in smart cities – Open data and smart cities – Data and access in smart cities – Policy, governance and regulation in smart cities – Privacy and sharing in smart cities
Chapter 7	Innovation – Innovation and smart cities – Data and smart cities: collaboration, ownership and value
Chapter 8	Disruption – Disruption and smart cities – Collaboration, complexity and success in smart cities

cities. Chapter 6 focuses on openness and data in smart cities through a review of
the research literature for open data and smart cities; data and access in smart cities;
policy, governance, and regulation in smart cities; and privacy and sharing in smart
cities. Chapter 7 focuses on innovation through a review of the research literature
for innovation and smart cities; and then for data and smart cities—collaboration,
ownerships, and value. Chapter 8 focuses on disruption through a review of the
research literature for disruption and smart cities; and then for collaboration, complexity, and success in smart cities.

This review of the research literature enabled the identification of key factors for
exploration while revealing challenges and opportunities, as highlighted in Tables
9.3 and 9.4, respectively.

An overview of key challenges emerging from the literature reviews is provided
by chapter in Table 9.3. Of note across chapters in Table 9.3 is the presence of concerns with definitions; with involving people meaningfully in smart cities; and with
the human dimension more generally in terms of collaboration, data, imagination,
adaptability, and sustainability supported through various types of infrastructures.

An overview of key opportunities emerging from the literature reviews is provided by chapter in Table 9.4. Of note in Table 9.4 is the presence of elements such

Table 9.3 Key challenges for seeing through smart cities

Chapter	Key challenges
Chapter 1	Human-centric technologies; urban knowledge frameworks
Chapter 2	Privacy; appropriation of technologies; human-in-the-loop sensing
Chapter 3	(Methodological approach)
Chapter 4	Defining urban data; technologies that minimize awareness; device location
Chapter 5	Defining urban learning; learning infrastructures; people & data interactions
Chapter 6	Defining urban openness; openness infrastructures; people, privacy & data interactions
Chapter 7	Defining urban innovation; innovation infrastructures; people, imagination & data interactions
Chapter 8	Defining urban disruption; disruption infrastructures; adaptability, resilience & sustainability

Table 9.4 Key opportunities for seeing through smart cities

Chapter	Opportunities
Chapter 1	Disruptive digital data developments
Chapter 2	IoT device location; hacking as agency; urban meta-sensing
Chapter 3	(Methodological approach)
Chapter 4	Defining urban data; urban data collaborations; technology awareness
Chapter 5	Lifewide & lifelong literacies; learning infrastructures; data literacies
Chapter 6	Data access; openness infrastructures; data privacy architectures
Chapter 7	Imagination & data value; innovation infrastructure; collaboration, sharing & data visualizations
Chapter 8	Disruption & adaptability; disruption infrastructures; collaboration, complexity & success

Table 9.5 Literatures reviews: similarities and differences of factors by dimension

Factors	Similarities	Differences
Chapter 1—Smart cities	Digital data/layer Inverse infrastructures (self-org)	Ambient context Data & the end of theory High/low frequency cities
Chapters 2 and 3—Sensing	Actors assembling smartness Creativity Emotion/affect Hacking as agency Interaction & feeling	Appropriation by senses Appropriation of technologies Psychology of city living
Chapter 4—Awareness	Citizen participation (people) Collaboration	Device location (tech awareness)
Chapter 5—Learning	Creativity (citizens model) Data, information Knowledge infrastructures Privacy, security, trust	Ambient data Citizen engagement Informal learning Lifelong, lifewide learning
Chapter 6—Openness	Citizen participation Digital/data layer Government Interaction Policy Privacy	Interface & data layer
Chapter 7–Innovation	Assemblies of smart planning Citizen participation Collaboration Creativity Ecosystems (innovation) Hacking as heuristic, collaborative Imagination Information Knowledge Policy Social/sociable	AI influence on behavior
Chapter 8—Disruption	Collaboration Digital technologies Digital data/layer, information Ecosystems (urban) Government Self-organizing	Uncertainty Value co-creation

as agency; collaborations; imagination in relation to data use; infrastructures in support of learning, innovation, and the like; literacies, privacy, and other people-related factors within and across chapters.

Looking across the literature reviews in this book, Table 9.5 shows factors that emerge in terms of key similarities and differences. In summary, Table 9.5 shows key similarities for smart cities generally as pertaining to the digital/data layer and to inverse or self-organizing infrastructures which appear again for the *openness* and *disruption* dimensions, respectively. Across dimensions, similarities pertained to: *sensing* and actors assembling smartness, creativity, emotion/affect, hacking as agency, and interaction and feeling. Assemblies of smart planning appears for the *innovation* dimension; creativity appears again for the *learning* and *innovation* dimensions; while hacking appears for the *innovation* dimension as heuristic, collaborative; and interaction appears for the *openness* dimension. Citizen participation appears for the *awareness* dimension and also for the *openness* and *innovation* dimensions while collaboration appears for the *awareness* dimension and also for the *innovation* and *disruption* dimensions.

By contrast, key differences that emerged for smart cities pertained to ambient context, concerns with data and the end of theory, and high and low frequency cities. Across dimensions, differences pertained to: *sensing* and appropriation by the senses; appropriation of technologies, and the psychology of city living; *awareness* and technologies in relation to location of devices in the everyday world; *learning* and ambient data, citizen engagement, informal learning, and lifelong and lifewide learning; *openness* and the interface and data layer for the digital; *innovation* and the influence of artificial intelligence (AI) on behavior; and *disruption* and uncertainty and value co-creation.

The research questions formulated from a review of the research literature are provided by chapter in Table 9.6 and pertain to the dimension under exploration.

The research questions focus on people, data, value, and success and are reformulated as propositions under exploration in this book, as identified in Table 9.7, taking into consideration some of the challenges and opportunities highlighted.

The propositions explore factors related to each dimension involving people and their assessments; issues associated with ICTs such as privacy and trust; infrastructures for learning and knowledge; the value and uses for data along with associated issues of privacy, security, and trust; and the importance of adaptiveness, collaborations, and data visualizations.

The discussion of findings in Sect. 9.3 is intended to shed light on explorations of the propositions listed in Table 9.7.

Table 9.6 Research questions for seeing through smart cities

Chapter	Research questions
Chapter 1	(Introduction)
Chapter 2—Q1	Why is *sensing* as a way of *seeing* important for people in smart cities?
Chapter 3	(Methodological approach)
Chapter 4—Q2	Why is *awareness* important in relation to the generation of data in smart cities?
Chapter 5—Q3	How does *learning* pertain to data in smarter city initiatives?
Chapter 6—Q4	Why does *openness* matter for data access in smart cities?
Chapter 7—Q5	How does *innovation* as creative opportunity contribute to value in relation to data in the public realm?
Chapter 8—Q6	Why is *disruptiveness* important for success in smart cities?

Table 9.7 Propositions explored for seeing through smart cities

Chapter	Propositions
Chapter 1	(Introduction)
Chapters 2 and 3—P1	*Sensing* as a way of *seeing* is important for people in smart cities because this enables light to be shed on experiences, assessments, and visualizations of the urban for understanding, action, and success
Chapter 4—P2	*Awareness* is important in relation to the generation of data in smart cities in many ways, on many levels including the use of information and communication technologies (ICTs) and associated issues of privacy and trust
Chapter 5—P3	*Learning* pertains to data in smarter city initiatives on many levels, across many sectors including learning infrastructures and knowledge infrastructures associated with people and data privacy, security, and trust
Chapter 6—P4	*Openness* matters for data access in smart cities as data becomes more critical, complex, and valuable requiring ever more creativity associated with policy, governance, regulation, privacy, and connecting
Chapter 7—P5	*Innovation* as creative opportunity contributes to value in relation to data in the public realm in terms of potentials for smart cities such as visual ways to show success in real time
Chapter 8—P6	*Disruptiveness* is important for success in smart cities, associated as it is with opportunities for adaptiveness, collaborations, and the use of data to inform, educate, and inspire in real time

9.3   Findings and Discussion

Findings are presented in response to the research questions based on explorations of the corresponding propositions in terms of assessments of the dimensions of sensing, awareness, learning, openness, innovation, and disruption. Variables, correlations, and opportunities in smart cities and regions are presented in Sect. 9.3.1, what people said in Sect. 9.3.2, and insights and other aspects are shared in Sect. 9.3.3.

9.3.1   Variables, Correlations, and Opportunities in Smart Cities

Based on the dimensions explored in this work, correlations with associated factors are presented in Fig. 9.2 and opportunities are identified going forward in response to the propositions explored in this book for seeing through smart cities and regions.

Explorations of the *sensing* dimension where *attuning to urban spaces* is used as a proxy for sensing, show positive correlations with *walkability* at .36; with *livability* at .71; with *comfort* (e.g., emotion/affect) at .43; and with *interactive public spaces* at .71. Opportunities highlighted from the relationships emerging from correlations associated with *sensing* pertain to the digital and to data as less visible infrastructures as well as emotion/affect.

Dimensions	Sensing	Awareness	Learning	Openness	Innovation	Disruption
Factors	Attuning & Walkability	Awareness & ICTs	Community Participation & Privacy	Openness & Access to Public Data	Creative Opportunities & Meaningfulness	Adapting for Urban Uses & Collaborations
Correlations	.36	-.23	-.57	.77	.81	.94
Factors	Attuning & Livability	Awareness & Access to Public Data	Community Participation & Security	Openness & Privacy	Innovative Use of Data & Show Success	Adapting for Urban Uses & Data Visualizations
Correlations	.71	.23	-.57	.57	.57	.54
Factors	Attuning & Comfort	Trust	Community Participation & Trust	Openness & Trust	Innovative Use of Data & Meaningfulness	Adapting for Urban Uses & Show Success
Correlations	.43	-.54	-.33	.36	.57	.27
Factors	Attuning & Interactive Public Spaces	Privacy	Community Participation & Show Success	Openness & Connecting	Creative Opportunities & Access to Public Data	Collaborations & Data Visualizations
Correlations	.71	-.23	-.33	.63	.70	.57
Opportunities	• Digital / data • Emotion / affect	• Improving awareness for all items	• Improve trust, privacy, security show success	• Benefits/access • Improve trust	• Data value • Success	• Leverage data • The visual

Fig. 9.2   Key factors, correlations, and opportunities for seeing through smart cities

Explorations of the *awareness* dimension show a combination of negative, inverse and positive correlations with *ICTs* at $-.23$; *access to public data* at .23; with *trust* at $-.54$; and with *privacy* at $-.23$. Opportunities highlighted from the relationships emerging from these correlations associated with *awareness* pertain to improving awareness for all items—ICTs, access, trust, and privacy.

Explorations of the *learning* dimension where *community participation* is used as a proxy, show negative, inverse correlations with *privacy* at $-.57$; *security* at $-.57$; *trust* at $-.33$; and with *visual ways to show success in real time* at $-.33$. Opportunities highlighted from the relationships emerging from these correlations pertain to the potential for improvement for all items—trust, privacy, security, and visual ways to show success in real time—in relation to learning.

Explorations of the *openness* dimension show positive correlations with *access to public data* at .77; with *privacy* at .57; with *trust* at .36; and with *connecting* at .63. Opportunities highlighted from the relationships emerging from correlations associated with *openness* pertain to learning more about the benefits of *access to public data* while improving *trust*, to name a few.

Explorations of the *innovation* dimension using *creative opportunities* as a proxy, show positive correlations with *meaningfulness* at .81; and with *access to public data* at .70. Using *innovative use of data* as a proxy for *innovation* when correlated with *visual ways to show success in real time* a correlation of .57 emerges; and when correlated with *meaningfulness* the value of .57 emerges. Opportunities highlighted from the relationships emerging for correlations associated with *innovation* include the value of data, the benefits of access to public data, and being able to demonstrate success, dynamically.

Explorations of the *disruption* dimension using *adapting for urban uses* as a proxy show positive correlations with *collaborations* at .94; with *data visualizations that educate, inform, and inspire in real time* at .54; and with *visual ways to show success in real time* at 27. Using *collaborations* as a proxy for disruption, when correlated with *data visualizations that educate, inform, and inspire in real time* a correlation of .57 emerges. Opportunities highlighted from the relationships emerging from correlations associated with *disruption* include the leveraging of collaborations as well as data visualizations.

In summary, correlations range from negative or inverse for *learning*, using *community participation* as a proxy, and *trust* at −.33 to a "very good" [3] positive correlation at .71 between *sensing,* using *attuning to urban spaces* as a proxy, and *interactive public spaces.* To learn more about the quantitative findings from survey assessments and their correlations, Sect. 9.3.2 provides a glimpse of what people said, contributing to insights, spaces for dialogue, and the evolving of urban theory and methods for seeing through smart cities.

9.3.2   What People Said: Similarities and Differences

Looking across key elements emerging from interviews, open ended survey questions, and group and individual discussions, in terms of what people said, an analysis for key similarities and differences is presented in Table 9.8.

In summary, Table 9.8 shows key similarities to be the dynamic aspect for the *sensing* and *disruption* dimension; collaboration for the *learning* and *disruption* dimensions; data as serendipitous or accidental for the *learning* and *openness* dimension; clusters for the *innovation* and *disruption* dimensions; data visualizations for the *awareness, innovation,* and *disruption* dimensions, and so on. By contrast, key differences for the *sensing* dimension emerge as smartness as nothing visible in smart cities and the visual sense of the city. For the *awareness* dimension, ambient connection and ambient data emerge while for the *learning* dimension what emerges is the suggestion that "schools open their walls", using technologies to experience the city, geofenced content for community interactions, and learning as continuous. For the *openness* dimension, freedom and performance tracking emerges while for the *innovation* dimension open events emerge and data engagement for success, documented engagement, and uncertain futures emerge for the *disruption* dimension. It is worth noting that for de Haan, Haartsen, and Strijker [4], perceived success was found "as long as citizens are continuously active and in charge" of initiatives.

Table 9.8 Qualitative findings: similarities and differences of factors by dimension

Factors	Similarities	Differences
Chapter 1—Smart cities	–	–
Chapters 2 and 3—Sensing	Feeling of dynamic Human activity citizen-centric Multi layers of senses Physical & digital layers Urban displays (interactive) Tech as purposeful urban apps	Smartness as nothing visible Visual sense of the city
Chapter 4—Awareness	Tech awareness & city size Visualization of urban data	Ambient connection Ambient data (suggestive of)
Chapter 5—Learning	Accidental data collection-city Cities as learning ecologies City as immature in data sense Collaborations across sectors Community weaving Interconnections with cities Learning capabilities—strategy Participation trust relationships	"Schools open their walls" Using tech to experience the city in a different way Geofenced content for community interactions Learning as continuous
Chapter 6—Openness	City as playful open territory Data as open and shared Data as serendipitous accidental Interactive urban elements-city Social media & data streams	Freedom Performance tracking
Chapter 7—Innovation	City apps for open innovation Creative use of data examples Creativity & clusters Data visualization in real time Smart: Social, useful, purpose	Open innovation events
Chapter 8—Disruption	Clusters for collaboration Dynamic Inverse infrastructure—LFLibs Urban displays + data visuals	Data engagement for success Documented engagement—SM Uncertain future

9.3.3 Insights, Patterns, Spaces for Dialogue & Theory & Methods

The analysis of explorations conducted in relation to the six dimensions for seeing through smart cities in this book enables identification of key insights, patterns, spaces for dialogue, and implications for theory and methods and going forward, as presented in Tables 9.9, 9.10, 9.11, and 9.12, respectively. Organized by dimension, Table 9.9 presents key insights emerging from this book pertaining to people and their multisensorial capabilities for the sensing dimension.

For the other dimensions, the outcomes for correlations conducted between the dimension explored based on assessments made by people on factors for each is highlighted. For example, *awareness* when correlated with ICTs shows a negative, inverse correlation and positive correlation with access to public data. *Learning* shows negative, inverse results when correlated with a number of data related factors. *Openness* shows a "very good" positive correlation with access to public data, as does *innovation* when correlated with meaningfulness, while *disruption* show a positive correlation with factors pertaining to data visualizations.

Key patterns that emerged through the explorations in this book are presented in Table 9.10, organized by dimension. For sensing, key patterns pertain to emotion/

Table 9.9 Insights from dimensions explored for seeing through smart cities

Dimensions	Insights
Sensing	Aware people & their multisensorial capabilities in aware environments
Awareness	Nature of relationship between awareness & ICTs as negative, inverse (−.23)
	The relationship between awareness & access to public data as positive (.23)
Learning	Nature of the relationship between learning & data factors as negative, inverse
Openness	The "very good" + correlation between openness & access to public data
Innovation	The "very good" positive correlation between innovation & meaningfulness
Disruption	The nature of the relationship between disruption & data visualizations

Table 9.10 Patterns from dimensions explored for seeing through smart cities

Dimensions	Patterns
Sensing	Emotion/affect in urban spaces; sensing as acting & influencing by people
Awareness	Issues associated with ICTs, privacy, trust & access to public data
Learning	Negative, inverse correlations between learning and data related factors
Openness	Trust as a challenge for openness as well as privacy in tech-aware spaces
Innovation	Positive correlation between innovation and data related factors
Disruption	Positive correlations between disruption and other data visualizations

Table 9.11 Patterns for success based on dimensions for seeing through smart cities

SC & dimensions	Livability	Platforms (digital)	Value
Chapter 1—Smart cities	Density-optimal	Trust	Urban data
Chapters 2 and 3—Sensing	Comfort	Trust + tech	Emotion/affect
Chapter 4—Awareness	People + tech	Trust	Human element
Chapter 5—Learning	Knowledge	Sharing; social	Data
Chapter 6—Openness	Privacy	Trust	Urban data sharing
Chapter 7—Innovation	Economy	Privacy; trust	Creativity
Chapter 8—Disruption	Remote working	Decentralization	Adaptability

Table 9.12 Spaces for dialogue from dimensions for seeing through smart cities

Dimensions	Spaces for dialogue
Sensing	People & their multi-sensing capabilities influencing urban design & planning
Awareness	People & their awareness of ICTs & data influencing urban design & planning
Learning	Meaningful community participation as learning influencing SC initiatives
Openness	People & privacy & trust influencing approaches to urban public data
Innovation	People & collaborations in relation to innovation influencing SC initiatives
Disruption	People collaborating as an element of disruption influencing SC success

affect in urban spaces such as feelings of comfort (e.g., emotion/affect) as well as sensing as a form of agency, as in, acting and influencing by people.

For awareness, key patterns pertain to issues associated with ICTs, access to public data, privacy, and trust. For learning, key patterns pertain to negative, inverse correlations with data related factors. For openness, key patterns pertain to challenges associated with trust and privacy in technology-aware environments. For innovation, key patterns pertain to positive correlations with data related factors while for disruption, key patterns pertain to positive correlations with data visualizations such as those that educate, inform, and inspire in real time.

Patterns for Success in Smart Cities Patterns for success in smart cities can be many and varied and may pertain to the city itself where, for example, a community member (Chap. 2) spoke of "the visual sense of the city" as a way "of differentiating itself in a deeper way." From the learning dimension (Chap. 5) perspective, the importance of knowledge infrastructures emerges as reported on by Borgman et al. [5, 6] and it is worth noting the work by Laurini [7] in terms of bundles or "bunches of knowledge" defined as "experiments made in other territories or cities" that "can be modeled and stored as external good practices", contributing possibly to the notion of smarter people in smart environments and cities, or to societies of knowledge. Indeed, infrastructures emerging in this work pertain to that for creativity and innovation (Chap. 7) for disruption (Chap. 8) and many of the six dimensions for seeing through smart cities, providing spaces through which to consider patterns for success. Regarding the sharing and platform economy for smart cities, the question raised by Vardi [8] concerning what to do about social media is noteworthy in terms of questions associated with the role and impacts of social, trust, privacy, and platforms for the sharing economy; remote working and digital nomads; and for infrastructures that support decentralization in and away from urban environments. As such, an overview of patterns for success based on the six dimensions for seeing through smart cities is presented in Table 9.11 in relation to livability, digital platforms, and value. For smart cities, the notion by Lehmann [9] of optimal density for livability is particularly timely in the current context of the global COVID-19 pandemic where space and density assume new meaning and requirements; trust in digital platforms becomes ever more crucial, as does value for urban data. For the sensing dimension, comfort emerges for livability, trust and technology for digital platforms, and in terms of value, emotion/affect. For the awareness dimension, people and technologies emerges for livability, trust for digital platforms, and in terms of value, the human element. For the learning dimension, knowledge emerges for livability, sharing and social for digital platforms, and in terms of value, data. For the openness dimension, privacy emerges as in just enough for livability, trust for digital platforms, and the value of urban data sharing. For the innovation dimension, rethinking economies emerges for livability, privacy and trust for digital platforms, and the value of creativity. For the disruption dimension, remote forms of working for livability emerges, decentralization enabled by digital platforms in support of anywhere/anytime and nomadic work practices, and the value of adaptability.

Spaces for dialogue that emerged in explorations of the six dimensions in this work are presented in Table 9.12.

For the sensing dimension, spaces for dialogue emerge in relation to people and their multi-sensing capabilities, influencing urban design and planning. For the awareness dimension, spaces for dialogue emerge in relation to people and their awareness of ICTs and data, influencing urban design and planning. For the learning dimension, spaces for dialogue emerge in relation to meaningful community participation, influencing smart city initiatives. For the openness dimension, spaces for dialogue emerge in terms of people and privacy and trust, influencing approaches to urban public data. For the innovation dimension, spaces for dialogue emerge in terms of people and collaborations, influencing smart city initiatives. For the disruption dimension, spaces for dialogue emerge in terms of people collaborating, influencing smart city success.

Key approaches relevant to urban theory and methods that emerged in explorations of the six dimensions in this work are presented in Table 9.13.

For the sensing dimension, key approaches relevant to urban theory and methods pertain to human multi sensorial capabilities in aware environments. For the awareness dimension, key approaches relevant to urban theory and methods pertain to the awareness of people in the context of aware technology environments. For the learning dimension, key approaches relevant to urban theory and methods feature the leveraging of technology-aware environments. For the openness dimension, key approaches relevant to urban theory and methods pertain to supportive infrastructures in technology-aware environments. For the innovation dimension, key approaches relevant to urban theory and methods pertain to the influence of

Table 9.13 Urban theory & methods: dimensions for seeing through smart cities

Dimensions	Urban theory and methods
Sensing	Approaches to multi sensorial capabilities in aware environments
Awareness	Approaches and awareness of people in aware technology environments
Learning	Approaches featuring learning in technology-aware environments
Openness	Approaches to infrastructures for openness in tech-aware environments
Innovation	Influence of infrastructures for innovation in tech-aware environments
Disruption	Visualizations of data to inform & influence in tech-aware environments

supportive infrastructures in technology-aware environment. For the disruption dimension, key approaches relevant to urban theory and methods pertain to visualizations of data that educate, inform, and inspire in real time and thus influence in technology-aware environments.

Taking into consideration the process nature of disruption as described by Christensen [2], together with the guidance by Naphade et al. [1] that smart cities require a decade to become so, the early-stage findings in this book may be evolving, requiring ongoing studies that employ a methodology that is longitudinal in nature. Such an approach may also involve the need for adjustments to include longitudinal coding [10]. As such, over time, a shifting in the correlations found in this book are likely to occur.

Indeed, the innovative, disruptive, adaptive, and dynamic nature of smart cities would seem to be key characteristics enabling responsiveness in the presence of uncertainty; the ability to pivot in the moment to changing requirements and needs; and the ability to recognize opportunities and reposition accordingly.

Exploring relationships between dimensions for seeing through smart cities, using Microsoft Excel, a correlation matrix is presented in Fig. 9.3 where *attuning to urban spaces* is used as a proxy for *sensing; community participation* is used as a proxy for *learning; creative opportunities* is used as a proxy for innovation; and *technology driven services* is used as a proxy for disruption. The correlation matrix shows a negative, inverse relationships between sensing and awareness (−.49); between learning and awareness (−.52); between innovation and awareness (−.30); and between disruption and awareness (−.30).

Very high positive correlations emerge between learning and sensing (.94); innovation and sensing (.95); and innovation and learning (.96) where, according to Creswell, [3] correlations in the "range from .86 and above" may "actually measure the same underlying trait and should probably be combined in data analysis." A positive correlation emerges between openness and awareness (.30) and openness and sensing (.40); between learning and openness (.57); between disruption and learning (.57); between innovation and openness (.66); and between disruption and innovation (.66) where, according to Creswell [3], correlations in the .35–.65 range "are useful for limited prediction" while those in the .66–.85 range are said to be "very good" and those in the .20–.35 range are said to have "only a slight relationship" [3]. What is said to be a "very good" correlation by Creswell [3], emerges

	Sensing	Awareness	Learning	Openness	Innovation	Disruption
Sensing	1					
Awareness	-0.492366	1				
Learning	0.94280904	-0.52223297	1			
Openness	0.40824829	0.301511345	0.5773503	1		
Innovation	0.95257934	-0.30151134	0.9622504	0.66666667	1	
Disruption	0.81649658	-0.30151134	0.5773503	0	0.6666667	1

Fig. 9.3 Correlation matrix for dimensions of seeing through smart cities

between disruption and sensing (.81) while no correlation emerges at this time between disruption and openness (0).

These findings hold the potential for identifying important and emerging indicators for smart cities and more particularly, for indicators for success in smart cities. For example, the "very good" correlation between disruption and sensing (.81) would seem to highlight the importance of aware technologies and aware people in smart cities. The correlation between disruption and innovation (.66) serves to confirm an already existing relationship [2] while suggesting that this relationship persists in smart cities and environments. Also noteworthy is the "very good" correlation between innovation and openness (.66) reinforcing the importance of openness in smart cities, particularly in relation to innovation.

9.3.4   A Typology for Seeing Through Smart Cities

Based on the reviews of the research literature, together with the case study explorations and correlations conducted in the chapters of this book, a typology for seeing through smart cities is provided in Fig. 9.4.

The dimensions explored in this book for seeing through smart cities are positioned in a matrix in relation to a continuum of complexity and collaboration, from low to high. Based on the correlations presented in Fig. 9.3, the awareness and sensing dimensions are combined in the high complexity, low collaboration zone; innovation and disruption are combined in the high complexity and high collaboration zone; learning is positioned in the low complexity and low collaboration zone; and openness is positioned in the low complexity and high collaboration zone. For the awareness/sensing dimension, variables include interactive public spaces, livability, emotion/affect (e.g., comfort), access to public data, and trust. For the innovation/disruption dimension, variables include meaningfulness, data visualizations, visual ways to show success in real time, and access to public data. For the learning dimension, variables include privacy, security, trust, and visual ways to show success in real time. For the openness dimension, variables include privacy, connecting, trust, and access to public data.

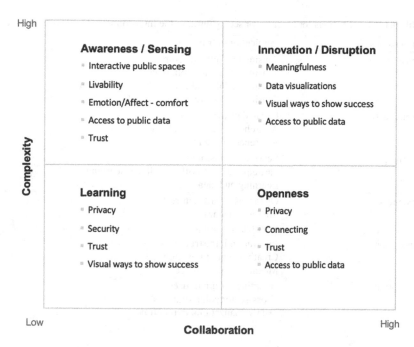

Fig. 9.4 Typology for seeing through smart cities

This typology may relate to and support the notion by Batty [11] of high and low frequency cities where change occurs more rapidly in the former and less rapidly in the latter, influencing urban theory. Typologies are said to be important for theory development [12] and as such, this typology opens discourse spaces for urban theory and for smart cities theory going forward.

9.4   Future Directions and Pathways for Success

Future directions and pathways for success in seeing through the six dimensions identified in this work as a lens for smart cities and regions are identified through implications for practice in Sect. 9.4.1, implications for research in Sect. 9.4.2, and selected after thoughts in Sect. 9.4.3.

9.4.1   Implications for Practice

Table 9.14 brings together a compilation of the implications identified in this book for practice, enabled by seeing through the lens of smart cities, organized by the six dimensions explored. For the sensing dimension, implications pertain to

Table 9.14 Implications for practice for seeing through the multi-dimensional lens of smart cities

Dimensions	Implications for practice
Sensing	Sensing and infrastructures Sensing and urban initiatives Sensing visible and less visible infrastructures Sensing through feelings of comfort
Awareness	Urban data awareness Awareness of aware technologies Awareness as seeing
Learning	Learning infrastructures Participation and collaboration as learning Learning and data
Openness	Openness infrastructures Smarter openness Smarter data usage
Innovation	Innovation infrastructures Creativity and innovation Meaningful data usage
Disruption	Adapting for urban uses Cross-sector collaborations Data visualizations in real time

infrastructures (including visible and less visible infrastructures), urban initiatives, and emotion/affect (e.g., feelings of comfort). For the awareness dimension, implications pertain to urban data, aware technologies, and awareness as seeing. For the learning dimension, implications pertain to resource infrastructures, participation and collaboration as learning, and data. For the openness dimension, implications pertain to supporting infrastructures, smarter approaches, and smarter data usage. For the innovation dimension, implications pertain again to infrastructures, creativity, and meaningful data usage.

For the disruption dimension, implications pertain to potentials and opportunities for adapting for urban uses, cross-sector collaborations, and data visualizations in real time.

9.4.2   Implications for Research

Table 9.15 brings together a compilation of the implications identified in this book for research, enabled by seeing through the lens of smart cities, organized by the six dimensions explored. For the sensing dimension, implications pertain to aware people and aware technologies, emotion/affect drawing on Anderson's Body Insight Scale (BIS) [13] as described in Chap. 2, less visible infrastructures for livability, seeing, and people and the real world in real time. For the awareness dimension, implications pertain to public data and potentials, seeing the less visible, and

Table 9.15 Implications for research for seeing through the multi-dimensional lens of smart cities

Dimensions	Implications for research
Sensing	Sensing and aware people and aware technologies Emotion/affect Sensing less visible infrastructures Sensing as seeing through smart cities People and real world, real time
Awareness	Awareness of public data and potentials Awareness as seeing the less visible Awareness: People, data, and technologies
Learning	Learning and aware technology environments Lifelong and lifewide learning Real world, real time data
Openness	Openness and data Data access, privacy, trust, and connecting Visualizing openness & exploring other data opportunities (e.g., neutrality)
Innovation	Innovation and data; innovation infrastructures Creative opportunities with a real world, real time focus
Disruption	Adaptability and collaborations in complex environments Visual ways to show success in real time Inverse infrastructures, resilience, and uncertainties in real time

people, data and technologies. For the learning dimension, implications pertain to aware technology environments, lifelong and lifewide learning, and real world, real time data. For the openness dimension, implications pertain data; data access, privacy, trust, and connecting; and visualizing openness and exploring other opportunities such as that associated with neutral survey responses. For the innovation dimension, implications pertain again to data, infrastructures, and creative opportunities with a real world, real time focus. For the disruption dimension, implications pertain to adaptability and collaborations in complex environments; visual ways to show success in real time; and inverse infrastructures, resilience, and living with uncertainties in real time.

9.4.3   After Thoughts

In terms of after thoughts, the importance of infrastructures in support of the six dimensions explored in this work—sensing, awareness, learning, openness, innovation, and disruption—emerge in both the literature reviews and in the study underlying this work. As such, infrastructures along with issues pertaining to data access, ownership, privacy, and trust, and other complexities emerge in this work through the literature reviews and in the qualitative data through people voicing their concerns, ideas, and suggestions. The emphasis on collaboration, creativity, and meaningful uses for urban data, while important in terms of patterns and relationships, also points the way toward future directions and pathways for success in a range of ways in smart cities and regions.

If, as noted in Chap. 1 of this book, smart cities provide "windows into the future" that "revitalize communities by considering how to improve human living spaces and values over time" [14], then findings that emerge from this work in terms of people-centered factors and the correlations, or lack thereof, may shed light on a range of elements providing direction and pathways for success, taking into consideration social and emotion/affect factors, the value of urban data, and livability.

9.5 Conclusion

This chapter provides an overview and discussion of the key elements explored in this book across the dimensions for seeing smart cities through the multi-dimensional lens of sensing, awareness, learning, openness, innovation, and disruption. A discussion and analysis of the main findings are also provided including correlations and patterns. From an overarching conceptual framework for seeing smart cities through a multi-dimensional lens to a component framework for each of the six dimensions, this work reveals emerging patterns and relationships as starting points for success in smart cities and regions. Focusing on the smart city characteristics of adaptability, complexity, dynamic, and collaborative, this work makes a contribution to the study and practice of smart cities in at least three ways, as follows: first, urban theory and smart cities theory are further developed and extended to include a conceptualization of dimensions for seeing smart cities; second, smart city theory is further developed with the addition of a typology for seeing through smart cities; and third, human sensory capabilities are explored through use of the BIS (Body Insight Scale) in the context of contemporary urban environments to complement the use of sensors and other aware technologies in improving livability, with the potential of adding value to urban data.

This work has implications going forward for: (a) practice, making recommendations related to each of the six dimensions: and (b) research, again making recommendations related to each of the six dimensions. A key take away from this work pertains to the correlations identified for people-centered factors in smart cities and regions, influencing directions and pathways for success. Also of note is the critical role of people in smart environments and the various types of infrastructures in support of the six dimensions for seeing through smart cities such as knowledge infrastructures, innovation infrastructures, disruption infrastructures (e.g., what Egyedi and Mehos, [15] refer to as inverse infrastructure), to name a few.

Regarding limitations of this work, understanding the nature of infrastructure more broadly than the physical in terms of city streets and so on provides a challenge for smart cities in support of smarter people incorporating infrastructures for digital data; human emotions, social interactions, embedded sensing, and other often difficult to see infrastructures, that were mitigated by the use of in-depth discussion and real world examples. The use of proxies for some of the six dimensions under exploration in this work was mitigated in part by including correlations for additional factors.

This work will be of interest to a broad audience including academics, students, city officials, business, community leaders and members, urban professionals and anyone concerned with understanding smart cities and regions taking into consideration people-centered factors for success on the one hand and seeing through the lens of smart cities using multiple dimensions, on the other hand. As such, three questions are raised for educators, students, and community leaders, as follows:

Q 9.1. Overall, what seems to be missing from this exploration of seeing through smart cities? And what would your key question or questions be?

Q 9.2. How would you describe one or more indicators of success in a smart city or region?

Q 9.3. Is success important for smart cities and regions? Please explain briefly why or why not.

If you would like to share your responses to these questions with the author of this book an online space is provided here [https://forms.gle/s3fVeaD8REo6ic467].

References

1. Naphade, M., Banavar, G., Harrison, C., Paraszczak, J., & Morris, R. (2011). Smarter cities and their innovation challenges. *Computer, 44*(6), 32–39. https://doi.org/10.1109/MC.2011.187
2. Dillon, K. (2020, February 4). Disruption 2020: An interview with Clayton M. Christensen. *MIT Sloan Management Review*. Retrieved October 11, 2020, from https://sloanreview.mit.edu/article/an-interview-with-clayton-m-christensen/?og=Disruption+2020+Horizontal
3. Creswell, J. W. (2018). *Educational research: Planning, conducting, and evaluating quantitative and qualitative research* (6th ed.). Boston, MA: Pearson.
4. de Haan, E., Meier, S., Haartsen, T., & Strijker, D. (2018). Defining 'success' of local citizens' initiatives in maintaining public services in rural areas: A professional's perspective. *Sociologia Ruralis, 58*(2), 312–330.
5. Borgman, C. L., Edwards, P. N., Jackson, S. J., Chalmers, M. K., Bowker, G. C., Ribes, D., ... Calvert, S. (2013). *Knowledge infrastructures: Intellectual frameworks and research challenges*. Report of a workshop sponsored by the National Science Foundation and the Sloan Foundation, University of Michigan School of Information, 25–28 May 2012.
6. Borgman, C. L., Darch, P. T., Pasquetto, I. V., & Wofford, M. F. (2020). *Our knowledge of knowledge infrastructures: Lessons learned and future directions*. Report of Knowledge Infrastructures Workshop, 5 June 2020, UCLA. Funded by the Alfred P. Sloan Foundation, Data and Computational Research Program.
7. Laurini, R. (2017). Towards smart urban planning through knowledge infrastructure. In *GEOProcessing 2017: The Ninth International Conference on Advanced Geographic Information Systems, Applications, and Services* (pp. 75–80).
8. Vardi, M. Y. (2020). What should be done about social media? *Communications of the ACM, 63*(11), 5. https://doi.org/10.1145/3424762
9. Lehmann, S. (2016). Sustainable urbanism: Toward a framework for quality and optimal density? *Future Cities & Environments, 2*(8), 1–29. https://doi.org/10.1186/s40984-016-0021-3
10. Saldaña, J. (2021). *The coding manual for qualitative researchers* (4th ed.). Los Angeles, CA: Sage.

11. Batty, M. (2020). Defining smart cities: High and low frequency cities, big data and urban theory. In K. S. Willis & A. Aurigi (Eds.), *The Routledge companion to smart cities* (pp. 51–60). London: Routledge.

12. Doty, D. H., & Glick, W. H. (1994). Typologies as a unique form of theory building: Toward improved understanding and modeling. *Academy of Management Review, 19*(2), 230–251.

13. Anderson, R. (2011). *Body insight scale.* Mind Garden Website. Retrieved July 11, 2020, from http://www.mindgarden.com/73-body-insight-scale#horizontalTab3

14. Forbes. (2019, December 23). Japan sparks new life in local communicates with human-centric smart cities. *Forbes*. Retrieved June 21, 2020, from https://www.forbes.com/sites/japan/2019/12/23/japan-sparks-new-life-in-local-communities-with-human-centric-smart-cities/#7d23f1a54398

15. Egyedi, T. M., & Mehos, D. C. (Eds.). (2012). *Inverse infrastructures: Disrupting networks from below*. Cheltenham, UK: Edward Elgar Pub.

Printed in the United States
by Baker & Taylor Publisher Services